TRAUMA REDEFINED

The following narration has been dedicated, with extreme gratitude to:

My loving parents, Ruby &
Rustom Taraporewala.
(My mom, my guardian Angel.
My dad, my pillar)

Edited by:

Ardavan Taraporewala.
(My son, who taught me how to write)

TRAUMA REDEFINED

PERVAIZ TARAPOREWALA

PARTRIDGE

This Book is Sponsored By

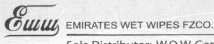

WORLD OF WIPES

Shields your hygiene...

About Us

IQI is an international property and investment company founded by a diverse range of partners from the UK, US, Malaysia & Singapore. Its headquarter is in Kuala Lumpur with offices located throughout Malaysia, Dubai, Melbourne and Singapore with strategic partners in South Korea, Australia and the United Kingdom. IQI believes in doing things different by embracing changes and constantly challenging tradition because of its strong desire to improve the way the industry operates. The company is uniquely geared towards offering an extensive range of property and services worldwide.

Combining local knowledge with global insight ensures that IQI maintains a structured and disciplined approach with the goal to create wealth for investors by sourcing for attractive assests and thus maximizing the return on investment.

Our Services

Secondary Market Sales, Rental & Management

We provide comprehensive & professional services to all customers across all types & classes of property such as:
- Advice & consultation
- Selection of suitable properties
- Viewing & inspection
- Financing

International Sales
- We source for interested investors & match them with quality property investments in favourable regions.
- To date we have identified and worked with a number of developers in Australia, the UK and Dubai and successfully marketed hundreds of units to Malaysian, Singaporean and Hong Kong investors.

Contact Us

IQI Holdings Malaysia
Suite 1, Floor 19, Wisma MCA, 163 Jalan Ampang
50450 Kuala Lumpur, Malaysia
Tel +(60) 3 2181 2820, +(60) 3 2035 6655
Fax +(60) 3 2161 0580, +(60) 3 2035 6656

IQI Properties Dubai
Al Moosa Tower 1, Level 3, 305, Sheikh Zayed Road
P. O. Box 9567, Dubai, UAE
Tel +(971) 4 352 474 8
Fax +(971) 4 352 474 3

IQI Bahrain
Office 28, Building 1684, Road 433
Manama Center 304, Kingdom of Bahrain
Tel +(97) 3330 17330
Whatsapp / Viber: +(97) 3363 23537

IQI Canada
144 Simcoe Street, Toronto, Ontario
Canada M5H 4E9
Tel +(1) 416 479 4488
Fax +(1) 416 408 0777

🌐 www.iqi-group.com
✉ hello@iqi-group.com
f facebook.com/iqigroup
🐦 twitter.com/iqigroup

To order additional copies of this book, contact
Toll Free 800 101 2657 (Singapore)
Toll Free 1 800 81 7340 (Malaysia)
orders.singapore@partridgepublishing.com

www.partridgepublishing.com/singapore

CONTENTS

INTRODUCTION

Dear readers, the events you are about to read are by no means written to "Traumatize" you in any way.

They are a true narration of events that occurred in the emirate of Sharjah, United Arab Emirates between 1:35 am and dawn on October 10th 2007, and the aftermath which continued for many moons. If you ever feel you have read a similar story, the coincidence would be uncanny, to say the least. No names, events and locations have been hidden; the following pages tell the whole truth even though you may be inclined to think that some of the descriptions are impossibly bizarre. Remember, truth, has always been stranger than fiction. I never paused to think about what to write; I simply gave words to my thoughts.

These events changed my life completely, and my personality took a revolutionary turn. They brought me close to the Almighty, and taught me valuable lessons, such as the importance of family bonding, of having good friends, the power of prayer, the power of faith, the power of love and above all, to conquer fear. So fasten your seatbelts and enjoy the ride.

If I try to thank my entire family and circle of friends for their indefatigable support throughout this ordeal, these pages will not be enough. With extreme gratitude, I dedicate this story to my loving parents Ruby and Rustom Taraporewala for being by my side in my darkest hour. My mom became by rock of Gibraltar; Dad, my pillar of strength.

To my younger brother Adil and his wife, Dr Natasha, I remain indebted for life. I'd like to especially thank Natasha; her own mother was critical in hospital in Karachi, and yet, Natasha would juggle between two countries and three young children to be by my side. I have no clue how to repay this debt.

To my own wife Mah-Zarin, daughter Nasha and son Ardavan – words fail me. It will take a lifetime to thank them. Their positivity surrounded me, with an impenetrable and completely impregnable shield of safety and virtue.

To my Lord I bow in gratitude, for giving me the family I have. Without them, I saw no future.

I also want to thank my employers, the entire Habib family, particularly the now late Reza Habib, and Zia Abbas Mirza and Adnan Fasih for their constant support and unprecedented care.

Thank you to my wife's colleagues at Emirates Airline, and my wife's now former boss, Tony Tayeh, for being instrumental in more ways than one towards my care and support.

Thank you to the management of Barclays Bank, for allowing my brother to be at my beck and call 24/7.

To all who travelled to the UAE to be with us – my aunt Roshan, and Pouruchisty Sidhwa, Adil Irani, Samad Khan and Behram Mana from Karachi, Pakistan, Tehmi from London, England, and Sam from Hamburg, Germany – their support remains unprecedented in my chronicles.

I will never be able to thank my dearest friends, Amin and Pooja, for all they did for us. They were by my family's side throughout the ordeal.

Thank you to Jade Baily, my publishing consultant from Partridge Publications, who has been instrumental towards the completion of this story. Her constant phone calls, valuable guidance, and ceaseless efforts will always be remembered with gratitude.

Jade hails from Cebu, a town in the Philippines. A strange coincidence; my daughter Nasha sourced this publisher for me. I have frequented the beautiful islands of Philippines in my quest for mountain climbing and have visited Tarlac and Antipolo. My love of animals took me to the amazing forest of Subic. And, as it turned out to be, my publisher came from the islands I fell in love with.

And finally a tribute to my special friend for this list would not be complete unless I mentioned Mehru Ardeshir Bhujwalla, my mother in law, although I'd hardly treat her as such. She was the grand old lady of our family. We all lovingly called her "Granny", and I'd fondly introduce her to my companions as my girlfriend. She would wear a permanent smile on her face, chuckling at my silly childish antics, and laughing heartily at all my ridiculous and mediocre jokes. Even in her mid-80s, she'd be the last to retire to the bedroom, ensuring first that the rest of the household had done so already. There were days when I'd come home in the wee hours of the morning, and she'd be at the kitchen table, patiently waiting and constantly praying. I'd walk in and put my hand on her head, she'd nod and smile, I'd proceed to bed, and she'd slowly follow.

Many prayers were held for me in different parts of the world. Family and friends had arranged ceremonies in Karachi, Lahore, London, Hamburg, Toronto, Tehran, Kabul and of course in Dubai. Granny didn't just pray, she leaned against God's doorbell, leaving Him with no choice but to open the doors of 'that best light' and shut the tunnel of darkness. With this kind of human pressure over the Lord's government, what could possibly go wrong? She left us for her Heavenly abode on April 6th 2014, leaving behind a legacy of love, light and laughter.

CHAPTER 1
THE NIGHT OF NO MOON

Numerology has relatively recently started to be recognized as science instead of superstition, and it plays a significant role in my life. Numbers, in general, are central to human existence. We have grown as a civilization to have our lives revolve around these digits. Our birthday is a combination of numbers. The first document ever created in our name, the birth certificate, is recorded via a number. Passports, ID cards, bank accounts, student enrolments… if we were to eliminate the numeric factors out of our lives, our very existence as a society would be compromised. My grandfather, the late Eruchshah Taraporewala, was a staunch believer in this science, and was himself a brilliant man of numbers. I used to spend countless hours in my childhood listening to his captivating lectures on these figures. It was without a doubt his passion for this pseudoscience that transcended into me. My fascination with this subject will show its relevance in a few paragraphs.

It was a hot afternoon on the 9th of October, 2007, during Ramadan, the Muslim period of fasting. A very dear friend of mine, Noori Malik, telephoned me.

"Hey buddy! Why don't you drive down to our place for dinner? My daughter has flown in from Lahore, she's an awesome cook!"

I was only too happy to agree. But I remembered that I had promised Ardavan that we'd stuff ourselves at the KFC all-you-can-eat Ramadan special. My son was curious to know how many pieces of chicken he could devour in one sitting. No harm done- all I had to do was take him and watch him eat for the both of us. So I went home to pick him up, along with my wife, Mah-Zarin, who managed to get roped into this too.

On arriving home, I greeted everyone, and casually announced that I'd be arriving home late from a friend's house that night. It was then that Mehru, my mother-in-law, hobbled silently towards me.

"Listen son, can you not keep this dinner for another day?"

"Why? What's the issue?" I quipped.

"Today is *amavas*."

"Today is what?"

"*Amavas*- the night of no moon," she explained. "It's not a good night son. Satan chooses nights such as this to do his work."

I couldn't help but laugh. "C'mon Mehru, do you really believe that the devil is lurking in the shadows, waiting for me?"

"Everything in life has always been a joke to you," she muttered, frowning at me. She was clearly unamused.

"Go to sleep," I said, as I kissed her cheek. "I'll be late. By the way, if good ol' Lucy does indeed show up, I'll call you and give him the phone. You may put in a good word for me," I added, grinning from ear to ear at my sarcasm. She simply walked away. I ushered Maz and

Ardavan into the car, we drove off to KFC, ate to our hearts' content (well, Ardavan did), and at about 8p.m, after dropping them back home, I was off to dinner.

Noori's apartment building might as well have been in the middle of nowhere. Enshrouded in pitch-black darkness, not even the flicker of a faulty streetlamp gave any light to the area. Not only that, but parking was a major issue under his building. I finally found a spot at a building that was under construction.

"Hey, what's your apartment number?" I called to ask, while getting out of the car.

"It's 251," he said.

Oh, dear God! Where the Hell are you going, Pervaiz?

My heart sank at the mention of that number, and my mind raced faster than the best horses at Ascot. My mother-in-law's Satan speech began to haunt my recollection as I realized that the digits of the apartment number added themselves up to 8.

This figure has never agreed with me. It has, in fact, been more or less instrumental in causing havoc in my life. Most of the time, if ever something has gone wrong, then the eighth digit of our number system has been directly or indirectly involved. (I trust the importance of my reference to numerology at the beginning of the chapter is now understood.) In spite of myself, I proceeded to Noori's apartment.

It was an absolute blast. We cracked jokes, exchanged stories, treated our ears to a tidal wave of glorious music, and above all, tickled our taste buds with Sidra's scrumptious meal. She is undoubtedly an outstanding cook. In all our mirth and merriment, we lost all track of time, and before we knew it, it was past 1:00a.m.

"Don't you work tomorrow Pervaiz?" Noori inquired.

"I sure do."

"Then please get the Hell out, because I do too," Noori said, laughing, as he got up to show me the door. I collected my things: CDs, phones, glasses, a flash drive and some books, and headed out of the door, thanking my hosts and wishing them a lovely day ahead.

After exiting the apartment building, I trudged along the pavement towards my car, which was about twenty feet away from me. Once more, I found myself in pitch black, without being able to see my hand in front of my face. And as Mehru had said, there was no moon either. Despite the eeriness of my surroundings, I found myself smiling at my good fortune. I had slipped through Satan's vice-like grip, and now planned on returning home without as much as a hiccough.

I had fun with my friends, the night is over, what could possibly go wrong now?

Plans…they're a funny concept- you create them, strategizing, coordinating every move, and yet, as if they have a mind of their own, they turn on you, and everything falls to pieces. My brother, Adil, once told me, "Pervaiz, if you ever want to make God laugh, tell him your future plans." That night, however, God was on a different platform altogether, and I was blissfully unaware of His own plans for me.

Suddenly, I tripped over a cobble stone, and all my belongings scattered across the concrete. My glasses, phones, keys, CDs, books all created a smorgasbord on the pavement. Sighing heavily with exhaustion and frustration, I scurried to retrieve everything in the darkness. Little did I know that within seconds, the events that were to transpire would change my life forever.

Chapter 2
The Impact

Just fifteen feet away from my car, I found myself face-down on the pavement. Not knowing what to think, at first I supposed the scaffolding above me collapsed, and the supported wall of the under-construction building had crumbled over me. My glasses had broken, and a piece of the lenses wedged itself above my left eyebrow. I thought my right shoulder would fall off any second.

The pain was immeasurable, beyond excruciating. I opened my eyes with great difficulty, but my vision was nothing but a hazy blur of red. Gasping for breath, I was greeted with the nauseating smell and smoke of exhaust fumes. Desperate to understand what had happened, I began rapidly blinking my eyes, trying to regain a sharper sense of sight. When the scene finally came back into focus, my eyes fell upon the bright red of tail and brake lights. Shimmering underneath them was an alpha-numeric scramble of Arabic and English on a rectangular metal plate, fixed on a creamy, off-white body. And finally, my eyes darted left. Right underneath the taillight were two glistening words that shone brighter than the neon lights of Times Square in New York- Toyota HiAce. That's when the awful reality dawned upon me- I had been run over by a roughly three-ton van.

What the fuck?! What have I done to deserve this? Was Mehru right? Was this the Master of Darkness, throwing his aces at me?

My thoughts then directed themselves to the driver.

To Hell with you, asshole!! Get out of the fucking van and help me, you miserable jerk!! How could you not see where you were going?? Are you drunk or asleep??

The wedged glass was still in my forehead, knifing its way deeper into my skin, until eventually, it was too much for me to handle.

Screw it!

Holding my breath, I pulled the damn thing out with my left hand. Big mistake. The floodgates of Hell opened up, and blood gushed out of the wound as I felt a staggering increase in the agony I was already being forced to endure.

Pervaiz, you idiot! As if shit wasn't bad enough already!

I could hardly keep my eyes open, as blood started sliding down and into my left eye.

Pervaiz, don't you dare lose your mind. Stay focused.

Seeing that his brake lights were on, I made the serious blunder of assuming that the driver was a good man, and had every intention of doing the right thing. But assumptions, as we know, are the mothers of all fuck-ups. I relaxed my guard, and with some God-sent renewed strength, I managed to turn myself over on my back.

He will surely help. No one has the nerve to do what he's done and not do a thing about it. But what's taking him so long to get out of the damn car??

With great effort, I managed to partly open my eyes, expecting to see the silhouette of the driver abandoning the vehicle and approaching me. But to my utmost horror, the unthinkable happened, and I saw his reverse lights switch on.

"ARE YOU TOTALLY OUT OF YOUR FUCKING MISERABLE MIND??!!" I yelled at him. I might as well have yelled it in my head. To my dismay, my loudest scream emerged as nothing more than a hoarse whisper. I watched in shock as the vehicle began to reverse. No surprises- he was trying to flee the scene. The blundering fool must have been scared out of his wits.

My blood had long since reached boiling point, and I felt like I had no more anger left in me to exude. My desperate attempts to gain his attention turned into pleading. A mixture of blood, sweat and tears of pain trickling down my face, I tried once more- "I'm still right behind you!"

It was more futile than the last, and I felt the sky-rocketing pressure of the van's weight on my chest.

CRACK!

I heard my own ribs shattering. With that, my mind went numb, except for the pain. I could feel and think of nothing else. Breathing became a Herculean task, and every ounce of my body felt engulfed in the most uncontrollable of blazes. Down to the core, every fiber in my body, every cell in my system began to writhe and shriek in agony, begging for relief.

But my pain, my fury, my desperation got the better of me. I was not going to let him get away with this, not without a fight. I realized that with the van reversing, I was being dragged into the middle of the road. Half my body was still under the van, and my legs were sprawled out in the open on the other side. Even God cannot decipher where I gathered the strength from, but as if acting of its own accord, my left arm grabbed his under carriage, with the intention of pulling off the vehicle's license plate. At least with that, they'd be able to trace the driver and see that justice was served. But it was not before I felt a searing heat shooting through my forearm that I noticed it was resting against the exhaust pipe. Silently shrieking, I felt the blistering, scorching temperature of the pipe peel the skin right off my arm.

That was enough for me. Unable to endure the intensity of the pain anymore, powerless to fight on, my body waived its white flag in surrender, and I released the under carriage from my grasp. There was nothing to do, but watch as he brought the van back onto the main road, leaving me in the middle of nowhere to die. He drove further and further away, until the weakest shimmers of the van's taillights disappeared into the darkness.

"Go to fucking Hell!" I croaked after him.

Control, Pervaiz. Stay in control, and stay calm. Do not worry, do not fear, and do not panic... Pervaiz, this could not really happening to you... this has not really happened to you!

But God damn it, it could, and it had. By now my white shirt had turned purple with blood. My face was drenched in a mixture of blood and sweat, and I was clueless as to the extent of damage done to me. Every bone in my body was screaming "Bloody murder!"

OK, Pervaiz, see if you can stand. GET UP!

My efforts were fruitless. No matter how many increasingly desperate signals my brain sent to my body, not a single muscle had any will left to move. The area was deserted, not a soul in sight. Darkness surrounded me, and the silence was deafening.

Some say Hell is located down below, beneath Heaven. Others claim the two places are across from each other. Both parties are seriously mistaken. Hell was right here, and I was in the deepest, darkest depths. Satan had the upper hand, and he played it exceedingly well. For the second time that night, I heard Mehru's words resound in my head. In spite of everything that happened, in spite of myself, I ironically found humor in them. I'll admit, the thought made me chuckle, but the laughter was short-lived, for I wasted no time in realizing just how painful it was to laugh.

Pervaiz, you were carrying two mobile phones when this happened. Where are they?

One, I realized, was in my shirt pocket. The other was somewhere on the pavement. Both were useless to me at this point, as I could not reach either of them. Meanwhile, my mind was racing with faint visions and glimpses of the events that transpired seconds ago.

Such is life...think, Pervaiz, think. What do you remember about the van? A faint vision came to my mind. *Artificial flowers... I remembered seeing the rear side of the van crammed with* plastic roses, sunflowers and money plants. *What about the license plate? Umm Al Quwain...*

That was all I could recall- the vehicle was registered in one of the more northern emirates. I never saw the driver's face. The only thing I was sure of was that he was most definitely not drunk. Sleeping on the wheel, maybe. He had his head firmly planted on his shoulders. Only someone in their right frame of mind would be able to drive over a human being, then reverse over him, and have the sense to vanish without a trace. I also have to admire his courage. His balls were made of brass, and his guts enforced with raw steel. He was faced with a choice- his life, or mine. It was just that simple. He'd be stupid to try and help a total stranger and be rewarded with a prison sentence. Ethical, but stupid nonetheless. Had he come to my aid, even if I was willing to show some mercy, the law would not be, and he obviously did not need to be told that.

My mind flooded with thoughts, which left and entered at will and at breakneck speed. Confused, unable to move, and in ruthless agony, I did not know what to do. I struggled to keep my eyes open, but my strength quickly faded, and like the shutters of a garage, they sealed themselves.

CHAPTER 3
THEN CAME A HUMAN

In the middle of a deserted roadside, I had absolutely no clue as to how to proceed. Still lost in a deep sea of thoughts, the one vision that would not leave my mind was the worst possible scenario; the hand the Fates would play if they wanted to be immeasurably cruel- a repeat of what had just happened. I was in the dark, and this time, on the ground, in an even more vulnerable position than I was before the first hit.

What if another Michael Schumacher-wannabe comes tearing down this deserted lane? No streetlights, no moonlight...Pervaiz, if his headlights don't catch you, you're roadkill. GET. THE. HELL. OUT. OF. THE. WAY.

But "How?" was the $6 million question. I could barely move, and my body was still too weak to try. Concluding that there was no point in keeping my eyes closed, I thought I'd might as well gain a better understanding of what, or who was around me. Squinting, a hazy and blurred vision was all my left eye would give me, and my right eye refused to open. I noticed, however, that my vision was being hindered by something trickling into my eye, as if I was crying in reverse. It took me a minute to realize that it was blood creeping in from the wound above. Mustering all the effort I could, I raised my left forearm so as to wipe away the blood from my eye. A Herculean task, I'd might as well have been lifting up the van that just ran me over. The burnt skin continued to peel off my forearm as I rubbed it against my eyebrow. I cursed under my breath.

But miracle of miracles, I heard something… footsteps…faint, but audible. As I started to regain some form of what was arguably vision, I saw a silhouette… a dark shadow approaching me…

May the Lord be praised- I'm not alone! Someone or something is here!

When the figure positioned itself at a ninety-degree angle opposite me on the pavement, I was able to discern it was a man. He was wearing a white *Shalwar Kameez*, a traditional Pakistani outfit. Craning his neck like a chicken trying to find its bearings, I could tell he was attempting to identify the object in the middle of the road.

"Don't just stand there buddy, come closer! I'm still alive, and I promise not to bite!" I beckoned, but at that level of audibility, I'd might as well have spoken in my head in a delusional frenzy. He simply stood there, motionless, studying me as if I was some Egyptian mummy that had escaped a cursed Pyramid tomb.

"HEY!" I yelled again- all the good it did me. "Please come here!"

He slowly and gingerly approached me.

"Listen…just pick me up and…take me to the pavement…I'm badly hurt…can't move an inch…"

The energy it took to talk…I felt my lungs would give way, but I needed to be able to communicate somehow. With great effort, I pointed towards the pavement. He looked at me from head to foot, examining me like an alien specimen about to be dissected.

"Love of God…stop staring at me! Take me back…pavement….*PAVEMENT…*" I pleaded, still pointing in its general direction.

Knowing fully well that I was, to an extent, incomprehensible, I was still furious and frustrated with his lack of understanding. I suppose this was more the anger at my current predicament that was bursting through. But then, to my utter surprise, he took a U-turn, and headed in the direction of the pavement towards which I was beckoning, leaving me right where he saw me. I felt my blood curdle. If my body had the strength, I would have walked right up to him and knocked the stupid clear out of him.

You idiot, TAKE ME WITH YOU!!!

On arrival, he readopted his motionless posture, and just stood on the pavement for a while.

Come on, move me to the side! Are you deaf as well as daft?

He started to move again.

Well, now we're getting somewhere.

Judging by his posture, he was searching for something. Finally, I saw him bend down and pick something off the ground. Seconds later, I heard the unmistakable sound of a Velcro flap being ripped open, and saw a rather bright glow emerging from his direction, like a light on a runway guiding a landing airplane. He had found my cellphone!

I felt my spirits soar as I heaved a sigh of relief. I wanted to jump for joy, but a 'thumbs up' is all my body had the strength to muster. I even felt my mouth twitch into what would have been a pathetic excuse for a smile.

"Bring…I'll give you…family's number… please call…thank you…"

But he just stood there, and for a moment, it seemed as if he was examining the phone more closely.

Are you trying to fucking guesstimate the resale value? Stop fooling around and bring it to me, God damn it! I don't have all the time in the world!

By now, I was completely breathless. Screaming at the top of my voice with only a whisper as the end result, was not only futile, but it was the fastest way to drain the little energy my body managed to retain. My lungs expanded less and less with each inhalation.

He started back towards me.

Glory be to God!

He stood himself near my head, and looked down at me again. My last attempt at communication resulted in hoarse whispers, wheezing and frantic hand gestures.

"Listen! Come closer, I can't scream anymore. I'll give you my wife's number. Please dial it and hold the phone to my ears. I'll do the rest."

I could hardly believe my eyes as he started back toward the pavement, my phone still in his hand. This had to be my eyes and brain playing tricks on me.

What the bloody fuck are you doing now? What must I do to get through to you? Please either help me or tell me you can't, just stop this ridiculous Tom and Jerry routine!

He turned to look at me one last time. What happened next made me question my sanity, and my faith in humanity. I watched in horror as he put the phone in his pocket and darted away from me, disappearing into the thin air out of which he seemed to have arrived.

This cannot possibly be happening right now, Pervaiz! This cannot be true!

And for a good few minutes, I simply refused to believe this scenario actually took place, despite being played out right before my eyes. This stranger, I assumed, was an angel in disguise, come to my aid when I needed him. But bless his heart, he turned out to be the very Devil, robbing me of my only lifeline- my phone.

Assumptions…remember what I said about them?

My favorite phone, all my contacts, appointments…he took everything with him. And then, it started. I don't know what got into me, but I found myself struggling to stop myself from laughing. Somewhere in all this drama, in spite of my ribs shrieking in pain and my lungs being moments away from collapsing, I found humor.

Pervaiz, my friend, you could very well be dead by the time someone else finds you, and you're distraught over the fact that your phone is gone? And what about that lunatic who needs a lesson in sign language and hand gestures (although there was only one gesture at this point in time that I felt the need to show him)*? Where did he come from? Where did he go?*

And that did it for me. As those words crossed my mind, 'Cotton-Eye Joe' started to play in my head. I could have hummed the melody had I not been chuckling.

In relentless agony, I laughed for what seemed like hours before I managed to regain control of myself. Still on the roadside, which was now back to its original state of desertedness, still too weak to move, I surrendered, indifferent to whatever could happen next.

Que sera, sera. Take a deep breath, Pervaiz, and trust in God. It might seem like you're in the middle of a rigged game of Trump, but if God is really as good as He's cracked up to be, take comfort in the fact that the house always wins.

CHAPTER 4

THE PAINKILLER

I had given up all hope of moving myself over to the pavement. My body just did not have the strength, and my brain had given up arguing with it. Thankfully, the one thing I would not relinquish control over was my state of consciousness. It definitely had its ups and downs in this situation, being conscious. I needed to stay alert, awake, and aware of my surroundings. All would be lost if I could not keep focus now. But the pain…the excruciating, agonizing torture…yes, it was my only source of assurance that I was still alive, but it had gone through the roof, and was growing more and more unbearable with each passing minute. I needed a painkiller, and I needed one now. But what over-the-counter medicine could possibly counter the torment caused by such extensive damage to my body? And even if such a miracle drug existed, what hope did I have of obtaining it?

Ok, Pervaiz, enough is enough. You need to do something about the pain before it ends up being the death of you. No more fun and laughter.

Fun and laughter…

If you can't figure out how to move from the middle of the road, at least try to ease the pain.

Fun and laughter…

Think, Pervaiz! The pain…THE PAIN!!!

FUN AND LAUGHTER.

And then it came to me- this little voice inside my head, uttering the same three words over and over like a broken tape-recorder, straining to make itself heard over the din of ear-splitting screams, was not trying to distract me. Rather, it was trying to suggest a remedy, one that I did not need to purchase from a pharmacy.

"Laughter is the best medicine." It's an old-age cliché, and now seemed like as good a time as any to put it to the test. With that, I found my mind wandering back to some of the best times of my life- the golden years of my childhood. Thinking about the pain would, if not make it more intolerable, do absolutely nothing for me, so it only made sense to allow my thoughts to frequent some more positive territory.

Mardan was my first stop. A small, remote village, northwest of Pakistan, at the foot of the Himalayas... this is where some of my fondest memories were born. I recalled our house-a lovely *Havailee,* a large villa within a village, where the untarnished and undisrupted wilderness was our backyard. Caterpillars, grass-hoppers and butterflies were my objects of fascination, and my best friends were foxes, ant-eaters and above all, wolves. My fondest memory of my encounters with these magnificent creatures came flooding back to me...a two year old toddler, sitting in the middle of a pack, surrounded by cubs who, in their innocence, took me for one of their own siblings, and watched over by mama or papa wolf...I was effectively living out Kipling's tales.

My mind then jumped to when I met the then President of Pakistan, Field Marshal Mohammed

Ayub Khan. It was at the inauguration of Khyber Tobacco Mills, for which my father was the factory manager. I was surprised to learn that I had the opportunity to attend such an event, where the guest of honor was the nation's President. He was a tall and hefty man. I could hardly see the top of his head if I tried looking up at him. But I remember our brief meeting as if it were only yesterday. Standing next to Dad, clutching his hand in mine, the President approached me. To my utter amazement, he bent down, looked into my eyes, and extended his hand saying, "How are you, young man?" Speechless and trembling with excitement, I could only offer my puppy paw in return. He chuckled and ruffled my hair as we shook, and his entourage beamed at me. He then proceeded to shake hands with my father, leaving me to bask in the glory of having the first handshake. I've never let Dad forget it.

Another memory I recall gracing my recollection was that of my grandparents, both maternal and paternal, and how I always looked forward to spending time with them. Dad's father, the late Eruchshah Taraporewala, from whom I obtained my obsession with numerology, was a kind, gentle and loving person. Whenever I'd visit, he'd have the brightest of smiles on his face, and always shook a firm hand. I remembered listening to his stories, mesmerized, hanging on his every word. And I'll never forget his sense of humor- his comicality was nothing short of endearing.

His bedridden state in his nineties had a deep, profound effect on me. It was depressing as a teenager, to see a man who was once so full of life to be reduced to such a pitiable position. But even in his sorry state, bless him, he never lost his funniness. I remembered one incident in particular, when he called me over, just to ask me, "What's for dinner tonight?"

I replied, "Dada, we have your favorite: mutton soup with boiled potato and toast.

Beaming at the idea, he pretended to roll down his sleeves, put on cufflinks, and don a tie.

"All set for dinner!" he announced to my amusement.

I chuckled. "Dada, you are going to have dinner in bed, and you want to doll up as if we were taking you to a five-star restaurant for a three-course gourmet meal?"

He sternly looked at me saying, "Son, never dine without a tie- you will develop serious indigestion."

We both laughed hysterically as my Uncle Jehangir brought him his dinner in bed. He then tucked a spotless white napkin under his collar button and thoroughly enjoyed every morsel, almost as much as I enjoyed feeding him, one spoon at a time. This proved to be routine until his day of passing.

And of course, there was my grandmother, or *Bapaijee* as I would call her. She was something, a real work of art. Plump as pudding, she'd strut around the house, poking her nose into anything and everything, whether it concerned her or not. And best of all, she lived by the motto, "Jesus is coming, look busy." I chuckled to myself as

I fondly remembered how she'd pretend to be occupied with all the work in the world, but was really up to absolutely nothing.

But above everything, I remember her stories. She could spin yarns of the sagas of kings and queens, witches and warlocks, fairies, magic and mystery that would keep me in suspense for days at length. Just as I thought the tale was approaching a climax, she'd leave me hanging, switching off the lights, telling me to go to sleep, and assuring me that she would continue the following week, provided I could remind her where we left off. This usually resulted in my retelling her half the story from the night before.

My mind now decided to pay my maternal grandparents a visit. My mother's father, the late Minocher Dastur, was a man who partook in the customs and traditions of the English more fervently than the English themselves. Short, extremely fair with silky white hair, I cannot recall ever seeing him out of his bedroom without his dressing gown, or out of the house without his three-piece suit and bowler hat, even in the blistering heat of August.

Every evening, he would come home from work, and we would sit side by side on a small, two-seater cane chair. This one instance, he held up his spotless, polished-to-perfection black shoes, in which one could very easily see one's reflection, and said, "Son, take a look at these. I bought them from the Bata Shoe Co. in January 1942."

"How come your never wear them Grandpa?" I asked curiously.

"Oh, I have worn them every single day since I bought them!"

It's 1967, and there's not a stitch out of place, nor a tear in the sole, nor a blemish on the surface...does he walk on thin air?

Grandpa came from a lineage of high priests, or *Dasturs*. He told me endless tales of how his father had sent him to a sort of monastery where he was to study the scriptures, and learn to live a priestly life, which was rather unfortunate as the idea never appealed to him to begin with. He would then chuckle, and tell me all about how, after endless pleading with his father, he finally escaped from that prison world, and humbly advised his teachers to kindly place their rosaries where even God wouldn't be tempted to look for them.

Chuckling at the thought, I recalled my grandmother, Putlamai Dastur. She was bright, active, engaging, and just like Eruchshah, a comedian down to the core. I just loved the way she used to tell me, with great pride I might add, "You know son, I have studied till second grade. I failed third grade three times. After that, my dad said to me, 'Putlie, darling, enough schooling. I can no longer afford it. Stay at home, learn to knit and cook. That should be enough schooling for you.'" We'd laugh till our sides were sore, for upon examination of her knitting projects, and tasting of her dishes, everyone knew she was probably better off in school.

When all daughters were married, and Grandpa was no longer alive, she came to live with my mother's sister, my Aunt Roshan, and her husband, my Uncle Nadir Rustomjee, in their lovely, palatial home. It was here that Grandma saw herself change from a village joker into an aristocrat. Watching her attempting to eat gingerly with forks, spoons, knives, fancy napkins and other such dainty toys was nothing short of humorous and adorable.

Put together, my aunt and uncle could give the English aristocracy a run for their money. In fact, it was thanks to them my manners arguably have some sense of refinement. I could dine with the Queen if called to do so, but all said and done, I still love to eat with my fingers, wipe my hands on my jeans, and sit and sleep on the floor. You can take the boy out of the village, but you can't take the village out of the boy.

The very last memory that entered my mind that night was not particularly pleasant. I was with my grandfather, Minocher. I don't remember when he said these words to me, but I remember that it was out of the blues, not at all relevant to the conversation we were having at the time. Gazing into the distance, he said, "Son, if ever you go out to seek revenge, please make sure you dig two graves."

I was perplexed. "Sorry?"

"Never mind."

"But what do you mean?"

"You'll understand someday."

Honestly, I still don't think I understood what he meant, but now, as I lay on the ground, gambling with my life, I was able to make an educated guess.

Did Grandpa have a premonition? Pervaiz, if ever you do get out of this mess, will you really seek revenge? Do you really want to go after the man who has put you in this position?

It's a thought that continues to plague my mind, even to this day.

I couldn't believe it…it was working! I had actually forgotten to think about the pain, which was making my ordeal more bearable. All these memories of my loved ones, my young, carefree days…they had soothed the pain, even if by a negligible amount. I realized that I had a constant smile on my face as these thoughts raced through my mind at breakneck speed.

Pervaiz, don't let these thoughts escape you. They've proven to be an awesome painkiller. Keep them close, and trust that God will keep you safe in His care. It's only a matter of time now before help reaches you. Hold on- you've already come this far.

CHAPTER 5

THEN CAME GOD

I was more focused, calmer than I had managed to keep myself up till now. The blood from the wound above my eye had just about stopped flowing, and I could now open both eyes wide enough to see clearly. But I knew I couldn't afford to get too excited. I was still in the line of fire, and needed to get out of the middle of the road.

God, where in Heaven's name are you? I've had my fill of this game, what the bloody Hell is taking you so long? Don't tell me you're stuck in traffic!

My own wit and audacity amused me. Considering my situation, I surely wasn't in any position to be demanding, especially towards a Supreme Being.

But hold on a minute...what the Hell is that? Shining... in the distance...

My heart started pounding uncontrollably-headlights...drawing nearer and nearer with each breath! And I recognized who they belonged to instantly- a Honda Accord. After owning the same car for roughly a decade, there could be no mistaking it.

Fantastic, just fan-fucking-tastic...Pervaiz, if this guy does not see you on time, you can kiss your butt goodbye. God, if you really are who they say you are, get here before the Accord does.

I knew I sounded rude inside my own head, but at that point in time, I couldn't care less.

As it turned out, however, neither did God. As the car drew nearer, my eyes clamped shut, waiting for the second impact...it never came. Instead, I saw the headlights come to a sharp halt, and heard the unmistakable screech of tires against concrete. Strange are the ways of our Lord.

Two young men emerged from the car and ran towards me. One wore a white *kandura*, the traditional male outfit of the U.A.E. The other donned a white shirt and trousers. Both lads sat down on the road near my head.

About fucking time! I thank you, God, for sending help, but I must say, a speedier response would have been more than welcome.

"Sir, can you hear me? What happened to you?" They immediately placed their ears close to me, so as to hear my muffled whispers.

At last, a breakthrough!

I instantly thought of the previous bloke, and how, in his stupidity, he did not have the sense to do so much as that. But then again, he did make off with my phone…perhaps his daftness was not so much a lack of intelligence as it was cunning.

Heaving a sigh of relief and pointing towards my car, I said, "Please listen to me very carefully. The black Pajero you see under the building is mine. The keys are in my pocket. Please carry me to it, place me on the driving seat, strap me up, and start the engine. I'll take it from there."

Wondering if they heard me correctly, the boys exchanged confused looks with each other. The next thing I knew, all three of us broke out into laughter.

"Sir, you are in no condition to be moved from where you are, let alone drive," said the chap in the shirt. He was South Indian or so, judging by his accent. "Just relax, we have already called the Police, and the paramedics."

"OK my friend, thanks a million," I said, still chuckling to myself. I had to stop though; laughing still proved to be painful. To my pleasant surprise, one of them proceeded to wipe my sweaty forehead with a handkerchief and cold water.

"Sir, close your eyes and try to relax. We will stay with you till you are in an ambulance..." The words themselves had a lull of their own, and that was the last thing I remember them saying before my eyes shut themselves.

Try to relax indeed!

No more than 15 seconds could have passed when I felt the very ground from under me begin to tremble.

An earthquake? Now?? God, do be reasonable. Don't you think I've suffered enough for one night?

My eyes shut themselves in a panic, as my entire body began to shake like an aspen leaf in a storm. I felt as if I was in a high-speed escalator that was on its way up. Things came to a sudden halt, and I opened my eyes as slowly as I could.

I couldn't believe it…the pain…it was gone. Not diminishing, *gone*! I felt chirpier than a lark in spring! My muscles had renewed strength and all motion was effortless. Excitedly, I put my hand to the wound above my eyebrow and caressed it. Looking back at my hand, there was not a trace of blood. It was only then that I realized that I was no longer lying on the ground. I was on my feet, fit as a fiddle!

What on Earth just happened? But then, do I really care at this point?

If only I could afford not to, as I soon understood this euphoric feeling came at a very high cost. I looked down, and could have jumped out of my skin at the sight before me. That is, if I was still inside my skin to begin with.

I was roughly twenty feet above ground level and the scenario below me was nothing short of horrifying. I was lying on the ground, just as I was a few moments ago...or at least, my body was. The two gentlemen were hovering over me, like a mother and father over their newborn son.

God damn it, how can I be in two places at once? How could I have an aerial view of my own bod? Am I losing my mind...? Hallucinating...? Dead...?

I remembered, being the ardent reader I was and am, coming across reports of apparently paranormal happenings, and read and watched interviews of peoples' out-of-body experiences. Is that what was happening to me? Was I seconds away from sprouting wings and a halo (or red horns and a barbed tail, whichever God thought suited me better)?

God, what the fuck do you think you are doing?

I would not have been surprised if, by now, I'd felt horns sprouting out from the sides of my head like beanstalks. I could not believe my own audacity addressing God in such a manner, but I didn't care; I'm not what you'd call 'God-fearing'.

You'd better be listening to me right now. If you think I'm afraid of you and your antics, then you are sadly mistaken!

In a panic, I turned my attention back to the happenings beneath me, and watched as two police cars and an ambulance arrived on the scene. My body was now surrounded by police officers and the paramedics, some of whom were pulling out tubes and an oxygen cylinder. I momentarily forgot about how angry I was with God, and the commotion under me kept me captivated.

"Sir, if you can hear me, take a deep breath and relax," said one of the paramedics.

"Who the fuck are you talking to?" I yelled from above. "Look up, jackass, I'm up here! That's a dead body in front of you!" I may as well have been talking to walls.

"Get the crash cart!"

"We're losing him, there's hardly any pulse!"

I couldn't help but laugh.

Crash cart? You imbecile, you want to jump start a corpse? Are you insane? Hold the crash cart till I hitch a ride back to my body, you twit. Don't waste your time!

God…God…where was God? Why was He taking His sweet time despite my desperate cries for help?

I know exactly where I am, and I know what you have done. God, I fear neither you nor death, but it is not my time. I'm in no mood to die!

Just then, I felt an arm around my back, resting a hand upon my right shoulder, as in a warm, comforting embrace of assurance. I looked at my right shoulder, and raised my left hand to it, but saw and felt nothing. Yet, there was something there, no doubt of it. The very thought sent shivers down my spine. If this was who I thought it was, the only person it could be, now would be a good time to choose my next words very carefully. Out of nowhere, a tidal wave of humility washed over me.

Please, just hear me out...you have given me a wife far beyond compare...you have blessed me with two of the world's greatest kids...my Princess Nasha...aspiring to carve a niche for herself in the ruthless corporate world...my son, Ardavan, whom you've granted a beautiful voice...I need to see his name in lights on Broadway, or in London's West End, where his shows will be sold out for weeks at a time...I need my moment Lord.

I need to be at a ticket booth, asking for two tickets to Ardavan's show that very evening. I also want the sales agent to tell me, 'Sir, I am sorry, we have nothing for sale for the next two weeks'. This, and only this will be 'My Moment'. Please, please get me that escalator back to my body...

"Shhh..."

A gentle whisper, soft, yet authoritative, ordered my silence, and demanded I pay close attention to the mayhem below me. As I shifted my focus back to the paramedics, the hand that rested on my shoulder was lifted. They were running to and from the ambulance like headless chickens, still trying to revive me.

Stop wasting energy over a corpse.

It started- another massive earthquake. Whether one of such magnitude had ever been recorded is highly doubtful. Seconds later, like a skydiver with a faulty parachute, I started to freefall.

Merciful Heavens, what on Earth is He up to now?

But I had no time to ponder an answer, for with all the force of a typhoon, the pain shot back through my body and every nerve in my body screamed in protest.

If the opposite took place when I was separated from my body, then that must mean...

I opened my eyes. The paramedic was yelling at the top of his lungs, right into my ear.

"SIR! SIR! TALK TO ME! CAN YOU HEAR ME?"

"Well, you've successfully robbed me of whatever hearing I had left, so congratulations!

Shut the fuck up and put that crash cart away. You won't be needing it now!" I yelled back at him in a hoarse whisper.

Just then an oxygen mask fell on my face. I closed my eyes. From that moment on, I knew for certain that I'd get out of this alive. I was sure that the relationship I'd have with my grandchildren would mirror the one I shared with my own grandparents, for the stories would be endless. They hoisted me onto a stretcher and wheeled me into the ambulance. The sirens started as a police officer shut the backdoors of the ambulance and sat by my side.

Seemingly rescued and safe at this point in time, I had no idea that the worst was far from over. Satan had only dealt the first round of horror, and the nightmare had just begun. For now, however, I took comfort in the fact that I was in His care. I thought about how ruthlessly demanding I had been toward God that night, and how, despite my displeasure, He showed me leniency. Maybe the time had come to show Him some gratitude instead.

CHAPTER 6

ENTER THE MAN
OF MEDICINE

When you are in light, everyone and everything follows you. When you are in darkness, your own shadow will not grace you with its company.

As we left the scene in the ambulance, I felt as if I had, by the grace of God, won some kind of epic battle. A feeling of triumph and positivity took me over.

I just might get through this after all.

Before I could contemplate any further though, Inspector Ahmed brought his ears close to my lips.

"Brother, can you tell me what happened?" he asked, in a typical Arabian accent. I had not so much as opened my mouth to reply when another oxygen mask was placed on my face. I ripped it off with my left hand, rounding on the startled paramedic.

"Look, I'm trying to have conversation here. Could you please keep your toys with you?"

"Sir, you have to get some oxygen," he quivered. It took me a while, but I was finally able to make him understand that my talking to the officer was more important than getting oxygen at that point in time, to me at least.

Slowly and in intense pain, I relived the entire nightmare for Inspector Ahmed, one step at a time, and he hung on my every word. When I was done, I gave him my wallet, car keys, house keys, and Nasha's and Maz's contact numbers. The inspector then put his hand on my forehead, caressing it, as if I was his own son.

"You are very strong, Mister Pervaiz. *Insh'Allah* (God-willing), you will be ok. Allah is great, don't worry. Just try to sleep."

Whap!

The mask fell on my face again. I smiled and closed my eyes, having no strength to argue. But not even two seconds had passed when I realized

I'd forgotten to ask where we were going. I removed the mask from my face again, much to the annoyance of the paramedics.

"Sir, you are making trouble for yourself!"

"Hold on a minute!" I snapped, equally annoyed. "Officer Ahmed, where are we going?"

"Al Qassimi Hospital Sharjah, brother," came the reply, with what I was sure was a slight snigger. He obviously found my childish antics with the paramedics amusing.

This is going to be a long, bumpy flight, Pervaiz. You'd better rest while you can. God knows what they'll tell you is the true extent of the damage at Qassimi.

With that final thought, I closed my eyes and thought no more, leaving the paramedic thanking God under his breath.

*

The next thing I knew, I was in some sort of a compact room, with machines, pipes and tubes beaming down at me. Six doctors surrounded me, three on either side. They all looked so stern, as if trying to solve the most complex medical riddle they had come across in their careers.

I'm glad you're all taking my predicament seriously, but would it kill you to smile? You're doctors, not immigration officers.

I was glad I had retained all senses, particularly my sense of humor. I just could not bear to move my limbs.

Pervaiz, listen carefully to what they are saying. Look around you and stay alert. Whatever pain you're in, deal with it, but do not lose consciousness and stay awake.

But the light above me was blinding, and I found myself squinting to provide my eyes with some shade. I had to close them.

Suddenly, I felt a slight pressure on my ribs, as if they were being massaged. I opened my eyes to see a doctor running his fingers against my body, feeling my ribs, abdomen, hips, and knees. Unaware that I had been watching him, and that I could hear every word he was mumbling, he made the greatest blunder of his life: he turned to his colleague and softly said, "This man has a maximum of twenty minutes left to live."

God alone knows what came over me, or where I got the strength from. With a mind of its own, my left arm grabbed his wrist, and locked it in a vice-like grip.

"In that case, my good doctor, use your twenty minutes wisely, I'll do what I will with mine," I hoarsely whispered to him.

Everyone in the room was paralyzed, and pin-drop silence ensued. The wax figurines of Madam Tussaud's London were livelier than the group staring at me. As for Dr. Twenty O' Minutes, his blanched visage made Snow White's face look smeared with grime. He wrenched his wrist from my grip, and that was the last I ever saw of him. I lay there, beaming like a kid in a candy store, immensely pleased with my success of having scared the lab-coat off him. It has been eight years to the incident, and I still find the story side-splittingly hilarious. I tried desperately to trace him, months after the incident, asking one doctor at Qassimi after another, but no one seemed able to divulge any further information on him.

A voice inside my head finally drowned out the laughter.

Merciful Heavens, Pervaiz! One fine day, your dark sense of humor will get either you or someone else killed. Now try to relax, for your sake, if no one else's.

Easier said than done. It seemed like no time at all had passed before all hell broke loose again. Before I knew it, nurses were scrambling around me in a panic. One was stitching the gash on my forehead, others were at work undressing me, and more were shoving tubes of all lengths and thicknesses into each and every inch of my body.

Suddenly, out of the blues, a soft hand landed on my forehead and caressed it. A tender female voice then whispered, "Uncle, you'll be ok…"

It was Sidra, Noori's daughter. To my delight, she had managed to sneak in somehow.

Before I could say a word, things started to get hazy. To my dismay, I started to lose awareness of my surroundings. I felt myself drifting away, and my mind now became flooded with fear and questions as I tried with all my might to stay focused.

What's going on? Why is this happening? How long am I going to be here? Where is my family? Has Officer Ahmed even informed them of what happened?

The following chapter contains the separate accounts of Mah-Zarin, Nasha and Ardavan. Mah-Zarin has a lengthier, more detailed story to tell, as she describes the events that took place while I was unable to express myself at The Qassimi Hospital. Nasha and Ardavan focus more on their own thoughts and emotions, rather than retelling the same story.

Chapter 7

Memoirs

I

It was Wednesday, October 10th 2007. Nasha found herself studying in my bedroom for her university midterm exam, which would take place in just a few hours. I awaited Pervaiz's return, so we could both call my cousin Tehmi, and wish her a happy birthday. Anxious to know when he'd come back, Nasha telephoned her father at around 1:00a.m, and he informed her that he'd be home within an hour. Nasha and I then decided to stay awake until that time, but after chatting amongst ourselves, we both fell asleep.

It seemed as if I had just closed my eyes when the phone began to ring. Rubbing my eyes, I stared at the clock on the wall. It was around 2:30a.m

"Mah-Zarin, Malik here. Pervaiz has met with an accident. They've taken him to Kuwaiti Hospital."

Words escaped me, and I felt my body go rigid with shock. Not knowing what to think, my mind raced to the year 1996, when Pervaiz and his friend, Nad-e-Ali, were involved in a car accident on the way to the valleys of Hatta. Whilst speeding against the burning hot tarmac, a tire burst, and the car spun mid-air three times before landing back on the ground. Pervaiz escaped death, but Nad-e-Ali was not so lucky. Was this a similar accident? Worse...?

No sooner did the phone call with Malik end, the phone rang again, this time from the Sharjah Police.

"Madam, your husband has met with an accident. You need to come to the Kuwaiti Hospital."

"Yes, I'm aware. I'm on my way," I replied, although how I managed to speak was beyond me. "How is my husband? What has happened to him?"

"*Insh'Allah* (God-willing) he will be OK," was all the officer would tell me. But that didn't answer my question.

"Can he talk? Let me speak to him."

"*Insh'Allah, Insh'Allah* he will make it," came the same words. They were hardly comforting, though I'm sure that was the intention behind them. I pressed on, insisting that they put me through to him.

"It is not possible because there is no network connection over there."

What the Hell does that mean? How can the difference of a few steps result in a loss of connection?

And that's when I realized- it wasn't that they didn't want me to talk to him- they didn't want him to strain himself while talking. The gravity of the situation now started to sink in as I hung up the phone. My arm lazily dropped to my side as I tried to process the scramble of information running through my head.

Nasha was by now wide awake, and fully aware of the situation, equally silenced by the horror of the story unfolding before her. I told her that I would go alone to the hospital, but she insisted on coming. Before I could argue, the phone rang a third time.

"Madam, this is Sharjah Police," said a man's voice.

How many reminders do they think I need?

"Yes, I know of the situation. I'm on my way."

"No Madam, don't go to Kuwaiti Hospital. We're taking him to The Qassimi Hospital in Sharjah."

"OK. I'll be there as soon as possible."

I still don't know what made them change their minds as to which hospital to admit him to. Maybe Qassimi was closer to the site than Kuwaiti, or perhaps better equipped to handle such cases…in any case, I'm just glad I was informed sooner than later.

Disturbed by all the commotion, my mother also arose from her sleep, and entered my room. I informed her of everything, and was only lucky she didn't have a heart attack on the spot, especially knowing how close she was to Pervaiz. Nasha and I rushed out of the house, leaving Ardavan sound asleep in his room. So blissfully unaware of the events, I so desperately wanted to leave my youngest child's peace intact. I decided against waking him up, a mistake I regret making even to this day.

II

Nasha called Pervaiz's brother, Adil, and our friend, Ali Gohar, to inform them of the situation. We reached the main road, desperately looking for a taxi. The first three cabs we hailed didn't know the location of the Qassimi Hospital, and seeing as we didn't either, we were stranded. At last, we made a breakthrough with the fourth taxi, whose driver managed to get us to our destination. On the way, Nasha continued informing our friends, Cyrus and Diana Magol, and Amin and Pooja Kazim, of what had happened. Meanwhile, a thought suddenly occurred to me that brought a lump to my throat.

I still had no idea about the nature of the accident. I gathered Pervaiz was hurt, but what else?

Was anyone else hurt? Was Pervaiz the reason the accident took place? Had he been reckless, or asleep behind the wheel? If he does make it out of this alive, is he looking at a jail term? Deportation? What exactly happened?

My world was crumbling to the ground as the worst of possibilities haunted my conscience.

Adil reached the hospital at approximately the same time we did. Noori Malik and his daughter Sidra, being residents of Sharjah, were the first to arrive, and met us at the door. Sidra informed me that she spoke to Pervaiz and that he would be fine, but I was unwilling to believe anything anyone said until I saw him for myself. As we entered the hospital we proceeded towards the police quarters and were met by Officer Ahmed, who informed us where Pervaiz had been taken.

He had been wheeled into the resuscitation room, which we were not permitted to enter. Not long after that, we were joined by Ali, Diana,

Cyrus, Amin, Pooja and the police. This time, I wasn't going to take 'no' for an answer. I walked right up to the men in uniform, demanding to know exactly what had happened to my husband.

"He's been run over by a van."

"Wh...what?" was the only word I could utter.

Thinking I would faint, they ushered me towards a chair. I didn't know how to react, and felt my mind go completely numb with disbelief. I lost my voice, my breathing became slow and heavy and my stomach was doing somersaults. I couldn't think of anything apart from the criticalness of Pervaiz's injuries.

How bad is the situation? Is he going to be alright?

The cops started to hand over all of Pervaiz's belongings that they were able to retrieve.

With nothing to do but wait, we decided to start calling our relatives overseas to inform them of what had happened. We first called Tehmi, but to our utmost disappointment, all we got was an automated voice message saying they were not in town. Next, I called Sheriar in Canada. Upon hearing what had happened, his cheery voice was shocked into a deafening silence. How I wished there was a way to break such news to my friends and family in a gentler manner. But alas, how could I have framed it?

Suddenly, Nasha came running up to me, announcing that Pervaiz would be passing through the corridor, on the way to an MRI and a CT scan. At that moment, I saw the nurses enter with a stretcher. Desperate to see the extent of the damage for myself, I raced against it. I caught but a glimpse of my husband, and the state he was in was nothing short of horrific. Unconscious, his face was caked in sand and blood. The intravenous tubes snaked their way around him like anacondas ready to kill. And his head, no, his entire body, was swollen up beyond belief. The nurses pushed him through a set of double doors, leaving me with that dreadful picture etched in my mind.

Nasha left the hospital with Cyrus and Diana to retrieve the car from Noori Malik's residential parking, leaving me to look after affairs in the hospital. Pervaiz was soon after transferred to the ICU. After a brief visit, we all gathered in the corridor of the emergency wing. A few minutes later, one of the doctors informed us that the test results appeared negative for any brain damage. A tidal wave of relief swooped over me, and I felt myself breathe again. A short silence followed, which Adil finally broke.

"Maz, you need to go home and sleep."

"What sleep do you want me to get, Adil?" I asked, without bothering to look up, rude as it may have seemed. "I'm in a living nightmare."

Calmly, but firmly, Adil pressed on. "Maz, there's nothing you can do for him right now, so I suggest you go home and try to get a few hours of rest."

Initially, I argued, but after coaxing from the rest of the group, I accepted Pooja and Amin's offer to drive me home.

The ride seemed to last a lifetime, but that provided me with the opportunity to rearrange my jumbled thoughts, and start prioritizing and putting things into perspective. Whatever God had in store for us, we had a lot to be grateful for, no doubt. To begin with, the test reports indicated no sign of brain damage. And of course, Pervaiz still had some life left in him, and that was all I could ask for. At that time, I made a vow that as long as he clung on to life, I'd cling on to hope, no matter how desperate and dismal the situation seemed.

III

I reached home at around 7:00a.m, and Nasha, who had arrived about forty-five minutes earlier, took off for university immediately. I found my mother with a prayer cap on her head and her book in her hand, as I would find her for many months to come. With ever vibrant affirmation, she told me, "Keep praying, he will be alright," as if she received a message from God Himself, ensuring Pervaiz's complete recovery. She was my rock in this trying time.

Ardavan was, to my surprise, asleep on my bed. I gently woke him up. In a groggy daze, he sat up and started to throw question after question at me.

"Mom, how's Dad?"

"I don't know, sweetheart. He's in hospital now. Did you just go to sleep?"

"No, I fell asleep around 4:00a.m or so. But what have the doctors said? How does he look?"

I told him all I knew, what Pervaiz looked like on the stretcher, and the results of his tests. Ardavan nodded in acknowledgement, and flopped back down on the bed.

"Honey, it's past 7:00a.m, you need to get dressed. You'll be late for school."

Ardavan looked at me as if I had suggested that two plus two equaled five. But I was adamant that he maintain whatever sense of routine he could to keep him distracted. He was probably too tired to argue. He silently got out of bed, changed, and Tinkerbell (our terrier) and I accompanied him to the school bus.

On returning home, I had intended to take a shower, but the phones, both landline and cell, were ringing off the hook. The first caller was

Pouruchisty, who was followed by Cashmira, both my childhood friends and with whom I share a very strong bond. Then Aunt Roshan, who I remember was crying bitterly over her nephew's predicament. Meantime, my mother took calls on the other line. The news started to spread like wildfire, and I found myself repeating the story every few minutes to people who wanted to hear it first hand, and offer their prayers and support.

The panic started to set in when I received a call from Adil back at the hospital.

"Maz, he can't breathe on his own. They've put him on an artificial respirator. My driver is on his way to collect you and bring you back."

My heart sank. The rug of hope I was standing on was being pulled out from underneath me. The lump in my throat returned, and that awful feeling in my stomach revisited me. But I remembered what I had promised myself and my children earlier, that as long as Pervaiz had life in him, I'd have hope in me. With every ounce of effort I could muster, I thought no more of my husband's worsened condition, and waited for Adil's driver to pick me up.

He arrived at about the same time when my friend and now ex-colleague from Emirates Airline, Darshana, came to visit me. Word had obviously reached my place of work. When she started to console me, however, I lost all composure and broke down. A volcano of emotion, all my pain, fears and frustrations erupted from me, and my brain finally started to comprehend the gravity of the situation my husband was facing. The fact that he was in the hospital, fighting for his life, and that I was powerless to help, began to painfully sink in, with each passing second. My eyes were like broken dams, and the tears gushed through them with fierce velocity.

Darshana somehow managed to calm me down, and insisted that we pick Ardavan up from school, and take him to the hospital. She maintained that he was no longer a child, and being Pervaiz's son, he should see his father, and know exactly what he and his family are in for. She convinced me. I realized at that point that it was wrong of me to not take my son to the hospital with me and Nasha, and that I was protecting him from absolutely nothing.

When we arrived at the school, we met with Humera Ibrahim, the upper years' senior supervisor. She called Ardavan out of his Math class. On seeing me, his face turned white with fear.

"Mom, what's happened?"

He had obviously jumped to the worst conclusion. Mrs. Ibrahim assured him he was simply going with me to the hospital, and that things had not escalated to the point he'd imagined. He darted back inside the classroom and emerged a second later with his backpack. We returned to the car and headed straight back to Sharjah. Upon arrival, Adil and I traded shifts of staying at the hospital. It was now his turn to go home and get some rest, if that were at all possible hereon.

IV

I began to meet with various doctors, and each of them affirmed just how critical Pervaiz's condition was. I finally got a clear picture of all the damage his body had taken. So far, majority of his ribs were completely broken, and the remaining few were severely fractured. The *humerus* in his right arm suffered particularly traumatic injury and needed a metal plate for support. There was extensive damage done to his teeth and jaws, and accounting for the other bones in his body that took damage, a total of twenty-eight bones had been broken, including a few of his vertebrae. His skin was badly burnt and bruised, he was quite swollen, and a breathing device did the job for him.

They had given him a critical phase of 72 hours within which he needed to show some sign of getting better, or at least stay in exactly the same state. With the body having undergone such strain already, there was no room for his condition to worsen. If that were to happen, there was practically no hope for a recovery. For now, just about the only thing they were able to do was sedate him with morphine to control the pain. The doctors also informed me that if he survived the ordeal, healing would be an extremely slow and patience-testing process; he was looking at a matter of months of hospitalization.

I wasted no time away from my husband. I'd spend every moment I could by his side, talking to him, telling him everything that was going on. I'd hold his hand, kiss and caress his forehead, pray aloud and tell him to pray simultaneously in his mind. I had the doctors' word that he could hear and understand everything that I said; he was just unable to respond due to the large doses of morphine he was given. When I had to leave the room, I would try to read his files and reports, whether I had the doctors' consent or not. There seemed to be no end to my questions for the staff, many of which pertained to reports which contained a great deal of medical jargon far beyond my understanding. I'm sure they tired of me, but they never showed it, and I was grateful to them for their patience.

The day following the accident, Pervaiz's parents, flew in from Karachi to see their son. They arrived at the hospital straight from the airport, and Adil escorted them to the ICU to see him. I can only imagine what a trying time it must have been for them in their old age.

And then, there was my own mother. As I did with Ardavan, I initially refused to take her to the hospital. I didn't want her to see Pervaiz in the state he was in, fearing she would have a breakdown. But after much insisting on her part, I finally took her to Qassimi to see her son-in-law. There she stood, calm, collected and confident that Pervaiz would make it out of this just fine. Undoubtedly, she was where I have got my strength from.

It was now the 17th of October, the day Pervaiz was scheduled to have the metal plate inserted in his forearm. Thankfully, it was not a risky surgery, and the plate was successfully placed. One of our greatest sources of comfort was visitations from our family and friends. Friends and colleagues from Pervaiz's workplace,

Habib Bank AG Zurich, and Emirates flocked the corridors of the hospital as and when news started to spread. Mrs. Ibrahim and Ms. Sabiha Baakza, the Head of the English Faculty from Ardavan's school, also dropped by, which was very considerate of them. It was an overwhelming outpour of support we received from so many people, including strangers, who over the period of years have become such good friends.

Apart from that, the days at Qassimi seemed to drag on for hours. Pervaiz's dependence on the artificial respirator continued, he remained unable to speak, and the amount of morphine that he was administered showed no signs of being reduced any time soon. The doctors and nurses were absolutely right about the healing process being 'patience-testing', for mine was being tried with each passing minute. But two days later was an especially brutal test to endure.

Pervaiz developed septicemia, a blood poisoning condition, which, if left untreated, could have proven fatal. More tubes wrapped themselves around him, and more machines and monitors were placed around his bed. And if that was not enough, as a double shock, he went into triple organ failure as a result of the disease. His kidneys, liver and lungs all stopped working as expected, and needed the support of machines to function. For a person in his condition, with the body already having undergone such trauma, the doctors almost gave up hope for any recovery when they detected it. As it was, his immune system was effectively non-existent, and to expect him to be able to put up a fight against this disease in his state was ludicrous. He was, however, still alive, and that was my only source of solace. While the doctors grew more concerned and convinced his days were numbered, I held fast to my beliefs that he would make a full recovery.

V

It had been apparent from the start that Qassimi would only be a temporary solution for Pervaiz, and that sooner or later, we would have to move him to another hospital. This was in no way a reflection on the quality of service we received there; Pervaiz was always well tended to, the doctors and nurses were patient and sympathetic, and more than capable. But as a hospital, Qassimi had no trauma unit, and so was not equipped to handle a case as extreme as his. In our search for a hospital that did handle trauma cases, one name sprung up multiple times: Rashid Hospital in Dubai. It was also highly recommended by our friends who happened to be in the medical field. We decided to keep this hospital in mind if we were to move Pervaiz out of Qassimi. Apart from being a trauma unit of considerable repute, it would also have been far easier to commute to a hospital within Dubai itself, rather than to another emirate on a daily basis.

But the need to move him came sooner than expected, for one day, I received some disturbing news from one of the doctors handling my husband's case.

"Madam, it's about the septicemia."

"Has it grown worse?" I asked anxiously.

"It will if we don't start treatment soon. We need your permission to start it."

I was bemused. "What do you mean? Why would I not give you my permission?"

"Your husband's condition is highly critical, and the medicine we need to administer to combat the septicemia is very potent. So potent, in fact, that it could end up playing havoc with an already severely damaged system."

"I'm sorry, I don't understand."

"We're not sure his body will be able to tolerate the medicine, so to speak. If it can, and the drugs combat the disease, well and good. If his body can't handle the drugs, his condition will worsen."

"In what way?" I could hardly breathe while the doctor explained the details of Pervaiz's predicament to me.

"It would most likely lead to hemorrhaging."

At this point in time, my heart could have provided the percussion to a death metal track. Trying to stay as calm as possible, I asked him more.

"OK, what if we waited to see what the medicine does? If it works, fine, if not, we try something else."

He dismally shook his head.

"I'm afraid it's not that simple. If he begins to internally bleed, it *will* prove fatal. There's no stopping the blood if it starts, not in his condition. He will not survive the ordeal."

The harsh reality finally started to sink in. I could hardly stand straight.

"So without the treatment, he will not survive, and with the treatment, there's a fifty percent chance he'll be dead…?" I concluded.

"Basically, yes," he replied, a frown upon his face. "So you need to think very carefully about how you want us to proceed, Mrs. Taraporewala. And if we are to administer the medication, we need to do so as soon as possible. We're running out of time, and I don't think he'd be able to go on for more than a few days at the most without it. I'm sorry."

Nodding courteously, he began to walk away, leaving me to ponder over the tidal wave of information and choices facing me. After a few steps however, he stopped dead in his tracks and headed back towards me.

"I forgot to mention- we're aware you've been thinking of moving Pervaiz to another hospital. If we start with the medicine here, no matter what the outcome, moving him will be out of the question. He will have to remain here. So if you're looking to switch hospitals, now would be the time to do so."

I nodded my head in understanding and gratitude for his patience. Words were getting caught in my throat.

VI

We knew Rashid Hospital had a renowned trauma unit and that it was definitely more accessible than Qassimi was. Pervaiz was running out of time, and I was running out of serenity. There was nothing for it; without making any prior appointment, Nasha, Natasha, Adil and I found ourselves in the office of Dr.

Mohammed Baqer M. Ali, a specialist physician and Head of Intensive Care at Rashid.

We wasted no time introducing ourselves. I dove right into Pervaiz's condition, shoved medical reports in his hands, and explained everything the doctor told me about the chances we'd need to take with medicine to counter the septicemia.

"Doctor, would you be able to treat him?"

He shook his head.

"He'd need to be admitted to Rashid. I'm not permitted to treat him if he's at any other facility. But I've taken on dozens of patients of his criticalness and worse. Judging by what you're telling me, and what the report says, I think I'd be able to treat him if he was moved here."

I breathed a sigh of relief. It was short-lived though, as a second later, his face expressed the realization of an unfortunate circumstance.

"But that won't happen so easily," he continued. "You'll need the permission of the hospital's Board of Governors to admit Pervaiz. Our ICU is completely occupied, you see."

This confused me. "But how will you take on a case with a full ICU on your hands, even if we did manage to get him admission?"

"I'll figure something out. But first things first- find a way to get him transferred."

"Where do I start?" I enquired. "How would I get him admission?"

"With connections" he said with a slight grin on his face."

"I'll do what I can. If we arranged for you to see him at Qassimi, would you be willing to do so?" I said.

"We can pick you up and drop you back whenever you're available, and of course, pay you whatever fees you would charge," Nasha pleaded, making no efforts to conceal her desperation.

"No, don't worry about that. I will come to Qassimi myself. There'll be no charge."

I couldn't believe my ears. He was sympathetic, sincere and extremely accommodating. I couldn't express my gratitude enough. He was proving to be an absolute gem; not just a doctor, but a God-sent angel. Finally, someone seemed confident that Pervaiz had a chance at recovery. I hardly expected smooth sailing from here on end, but I felt my out-of-control world slowly start to shift back into focus.

VII

True to his word, he met us at the Qassimi Hospital in Sharjah, at his own expense, the very same evening. He saw Pervaiz, took note of his condition and studied his files. Two hours later, he sat us down. What he said next made my heart skip a beat. Dr. Baqer Ali informed me that the reports of Pervaiz's condition were a lot worse than he anticipated.

"But you said you handled cases like his before," I protested in shock.

"I know I did," he said, rather apologetically, "but I had not expected his condition to deteriorate at such an exponential rate as it currently is."

"So does this mean you don't think you can treat him now?"

"No, it means that the odds are not in his favor. I thought they were when we last spoke, but now, after reviewing his latest reports, I'd say he has a thirty percent chance of making it out of this alive."

"I'll take it," I said hurriedly. "I'll take whatever chances you give us." Not that we were spoilt for choice.

"The first thing we need to do is get him admitted to Rashid," he continued. "I told you, unless he's a registered patient at the hospital, there's nothing I can do. Did you manage to get permission to get him admitted?"

"I've been unsuccessful so far," I said, shaking my head.

"You need to keep trying. Do whatever it takes, keep hounding them until they allow it."

"You mean to tell me that there's a chance he won't be admitted there?" I demanded, absolutely flabbergasted.

Maintaining his calm, he continued, "Unfortunately so. But don't lose hope yet, keep him at Qassimi for now, and I will do everything within my power to have your husband's case accepted at Rashid. Meanwhile, you need to pull whatever strings you have to do the same."

I sighed in despair. Shrugging my shoulders, I said, more to myself than to him, "What else can I do?"

He looked at me determinedly and said, "I promise you I'll do everything I can to make this happen, but I'm afraid I cannot promise results. We'll have to see what happens."

I had no choice in the matter, we both knew that. I could only be grateful that he was making an effort to get Pervaiz admitted into Rashid. I was determined to do the same. I knew of nothing else to do, save for pray with all my might that with each passing day, we were a step closer to getting a hospital transfer. Putting the thought aside momentarily, I proceeded to ask Dr. Baqer Ali about the medication Pervaiz was to be administered.

"His doctors are right- the medicine prescribed could potentially wreak havoc on his body. I can't prescribe any medication as he's not my patient. But since they need your permission to start any treatment, tell them that you want him started on this alternative drug."

He wrote down the name of the medicine on a piece of paper and handed it to me.

"It's not as potent as what they've prescribed, so it may not be as quick in combatting the disease, but at least you won't have to worry about any hemorrhaging in the process."

VIII

Dr. Baqer was right- getting permission for Pervaiz to be admitted was no easy task. So as to not create offence, I have decided to not include details of exactly how we managed to get Pervaiz admitted into Rashid Hospital. I can only say that things turned quite political, and if it wasn't for the influence of the Management of Emirates and the effort of colleagues at the Habib AG Zurich, the transfer would probably have never taken place. Also playing a major role in the move was Barclays, the bank Adil worked for, for which I'm truly thankful. As Dr. Baqer rightfully said, *connections* mean a lot nowadays.

My happiness was so overwhelming when the permission to admit him to Rashid was granted, I could have cried. I had never felt so relieved about anything before. Grinning from ear to ear, I thanked Dr. Baqer Ali for all his efforts over and over again like a broken tape recorder. Even the staff at Qassimi expressed their congratulations and happiness that Pervaiz could be moved to a hospital more capable of handling a condition such as his. The transfer took place on Tuesday, October 23rd.

As much as I wished it, I had to remind myself that all our troubles had not come to anywhere close to an end. It wouldn't be as if Rashid Hospital would be providing Pervaiz with a pill that could have him up and about like nothing had gone wrong. But far away from the end of the nightmare as we may have been, we were still a step closer to seeing it through.

There were ups and downs, even while he was at Rashid. But strange as it may seem, there were times when I'd be telling Dr. Baqer Ali not to worry, and that Pervaiz would make it through a bump in the road. I knew I'd have to remain positive throughout this ordeal, and see each development for what direction it was headed in, not its magnitude. Plus, I was nowhere near ready to let my husband go, or allow my children to lose their dad. I truly believe it was a positive attitude, in addition to prayers, and the medicines administered by a team of knowledgeable and supportive doctors that was key to Pervaiz's transfer from the ICU to the step-down ICU. It was at that point in time that his journey to recovery started to gain some momentum.

Nasha's Account

I

At the hospital, as soon as I knew where they had taken my father, I ran to see him for myself. At first, they didn't allow me in, but I couldn't care less. As soon as someone left the room, I wedged my foot through the door and peeked through. There he was, at the far end of the room. I could only catch a glimpse of him- he was covered in blood and sand. I raced back to the police quarters, where the cops were still discussing matters with Mom and Adil.

I was able to see Dad properly only once he was being wheeled out of the recovery room and taken for scans. He was so badly swollen that it seemed he had hardly any neck. His head was a football balancing on a pole. Initially, I questioned whether I was staring at my own father or someone else. Once it started to sink in that it was indeed him that I was looking at, my knees buckled. Had Adil not supported me from the left, and Mom from the right, I would have fallen.

II

Soon after, with the shoulders of my pullover soaked with Adil and Mom's tears, Cyrus, Diana and I went to the scene of the crime to retrieve our car. The darkness was unnerving. I was reminded about the stories my father would tell us, about mountain-climbing in Chitral, Northern Pakistan, where the darkness would not allow someone to see their hand in front of them. I had to try it for myself. I raised my hand to my face, and without exaggeration, I saw nothing. Cyrus drove the car back to my house and handed me the key, and then left in his own car with Diana. My friend picked me up and took me to university, for my economics exam the same morning.

That evening, I returned to the site with a couple of friends to ask around if anyone had any account of the events of the previous night, but not a soul knew what we were referring to.

Feeling defeated, we headed back to our car, but stopped dead in our tracks. Shimmering in the sunset were the remains of what was unmistakably a large puddle of blood. But this wasn't an ordinary pool; it had a more oblong shape with streaks, suggesting the victim had been dragged against the tarmac.

The phone calls we'd receive, the time we'd receive them, and from whom we'd receive them, over the next few days, became pretty standardized. Some would call once a day, others more often. Tehmi called every four hours, and being a medical professional herself, even taught me how to read Dad's vitals on the monitors surrounding him. These phone conversations would run like clockwork for quite some time.

I'd like to end by saying that the only person I knew who had unshaking and indestructible confidence in Dad's survival was Mom. The kind of courage she exemplified throughout the entire ordeal was unparalleled. Whether it was septicemia, the triple organ failure or worse, Mom was a rock, for all who loved Dad. I'm truly blessed to have such a strong woman for a mother.

Ardavan's Account

I

I woke up to the blinding bedroom light, which was enough to annoy and confuse me. I realized my grandmother was on the phone with someone. Turning my head towards the wall clock, I saw that it was around 3:00a.m

"Granny, what's happening? Who are you talking to?" I asked groggily, my eyes barely opening.

She ignored me. I got out of bed and sat next to her, poking her, using hand gestures, trying to get her attention. She finally gave me the phone, saying, "It's Ali."

"Ali who?"

"Ali Gohar. Dad's had an accident."

I put the phone to my ear. Sure enough, it was Ali.

"Ali, what on Earth is going on?" I asked, completely perplexed.

"Ardavan, Dad has had an accident."

"What accident? Is he alright?"

"He's been hit by a van."

I needed him to repeat himself, because the news just didn't register with me. I simply did not understand what was happening, and to whom.

"Where is he?"

"He's been taken to a hospital in Sharjah. *Insh'Allah*, he'll be alright."

"OK, where's Mom?"

"Mom and Nasha have gone to the hospital. They're on their way there."

I didn't know what to say. I forced the phone back into Granny's hand and proceeded towards the bathroom. While she continued the conversation with him, I locked myself behind the door, buried my face in my hands, slid to the floor and wept.

After about twenty minutes of silently crying, I realized I needed to check on my grandmother.

She had made her way to the kitchen, where I found her on her chair, praying rapidly and with furious concentration. I decided it was best to do the same. I went to the living room and said my prayers, tears flowing occasionally. By the time I was done praying, it was about 4:00a.m Unable to do or think any more, I proceeded to my mother's bed, hoping this was a bad dream, and that I'd wake up in my own room, with Dad telling me to hurry out of bed so as to not make him late for work the next day.

II

But it was not meant to be, as a few hours later, I found myself questioning my mother about the events that transpired the night before. She saw me onto my school bus, and then left to walk Tinkerbell. I took my usual seat next to the driver, and my tormentors began their usual routine of name-calling throughout the ride to school. Besides still trying to comprehend the happenings of the previous night, I was too tired to defend myself. I stared out of the window, trying my level best to contain my tears. Nasha's best friend's brother used to ride on the same bus. I don't know whether he knew at that point or not about Dad's situation, but he was the only one who stood up for me. It made no difference, and the bullies continued to ridicule me, but I was grateful nonetheless.

I made my way to my classroom, and quietly took my seat. My friends greeted me, but I didn't as much as look at them. Sensing something was wrong, my best friend, Rayomand Gilder, proceeded to ask me what the matter was. I didn't answer, but he probably knew from the look on my face that I was about to break down into tears. I lowered my head down onto my desk, doing whatever I could to hide my sorrow. My friends huddled around my desk, knelt down beside me, put their arms around me and tried to get me to tell them what was wrong. Eventually, I spoke.

"Dad's in the hospital."

There was a momentary silence. Rayomand was the first to speak.

"What happened?"

"He's been hit by a van."

He was stunned, as was the rest of the group. "What?"

"He's been hit by a van," I repeated. "He's critical."

Just then, our class teacher, Mrs. Menon, entered, and one of my classmates told her what happened. She stopped dead in her tracks, shocked into silence. With that, I lost all composure, pushed my way out of the group and headed to the washroom across the hall from my classroom. Both my teacher and Rayomand followed me. After somehow managing to calm me down, they escorted me back to the classroom. As the bell marking the beginning of first period rang, my friends offered their support and prayers for Dad's speedy recovery.

The rest of my day was interrupted by various teachers coming up to me, asking for details, offering sympathy or both, whether I was in the middle of a class or not. News had spread throughout the staffroom like wildfire, and I found myself repeating the story multiple times throughout the day.

Normally, it would have been a pleasant surprise to see Mom at school, but when I saw her at the end of the day, it came as more of a rude shock. I was quick to think that Dad didn't pull through, and that she had come to convey the bad news. But thankfully, she had come to take me to the hospital, a place I should have been hours ago. It was a long time before I forgave my mother for not waking me up that night and taking me with her and Nasha to Qassimi.

III

At the hospital, I met Adil, our family friends, and Mom's colleagues. They gathered around her, sat beside her on the sofas. And then, for the first time in my life, I saw my mother in tears. Unable to contain herself anymore, she had a complete breakdown. I did not know what to do. In my life, I had often been comforted by my mother, but I never found myself in a position where I had to comfort her. I simply stood across from the sofa she sat on, and left it up to her friends to provide her with solace.

I started getting emotional when we began to receive phone calls from people across the world. Ironically, hearing people say things such as, "He'll make it out of this," or "We're praying for him," or "Be strong, don't lose hope," and so on only made the situation worse. I suppose it reinforced the possibility that the exact opposite would happen, and that my father would *not* make it. I don't remember being able to answer a phone call without breaking out into tears myself, and having to shove the phone into someone else's hands. But truth be told, I'd rather people have not said things such as, "He'll be alright," because simply put, they had no way of confirming that. Even though I knew they were meant to be words of encouragement, they seemed foolishly optimistic at the time, and more like empty promises instead.

IV

Over time, while my father's condition began to worsen, I found my fear, sorrow and despair quickly metamorphosed into anger. My frustrations were mainly due to the fact that my father, my family and all our loved ones were being made to suffer an unfair ordeal. I was angry with the driver who ran Dad over, did nothing to help, and eventually managed to escape justice. I was furious at the fact that he managed to walk away from this with nothing but a guilty conscience (if he had one at all).

But more than anyone, I was angry with God, and it started to show. Over the course of time, I felt my faith in an all-loving, kind, generous deity slowly deteriorate. Prayers became more of a chore rather than a source of comfort. I never had a reason to question my faith before, but now my mind raced with queries to which I demanded answers.

God, how could you have allowed this to happen? Why did you allow the driver to get away? Are you punishing my father for something? What could he have possibly done to deserve this? Why punish so many people besides? Or are you punishing me for something? If so, why put my Dad through Hell?

I searched through many books on Zoroastrianism, our beliefs, our scriptures, desperate for answers. With the resources I had, I was unlucky, as I either did not find them, or did not find them satisfactory. I'd be concealing the truth if I didn't admit that I eventually began to question God's very existence. It's rather ironic that at a time when one would expect one's faith to be at its strongest, it was in fact the weakest it had ever been.

With my gradual loss of faith, I also found that my mind started to harbor some particularly ugly thoughts, mainly what I would do if I ever met the man responsible for my father's predicament. What would I say? Would I call for his execution? A life sentence? And then, my mind turned to what he did. He ran my father over twice with his van and left him for dead. Would I want the same to happen to him? Would 'justice' mean I would run him over with a van, leaving his life in the hands of God? Was I thinking about justice, or was this more along the lines of revenge? Did the two concepts ever meet common ground? Were these feelings of hatred and anger justified, understandable, morally corrupt…?

And finally, I believe this anecdote is worthy of mention. Despite what had happened, despite my father being critically ill in the hospital, fighting for his very life on a daily basis, I found myself being able to engage in activities that would make one question whether I fully grasped the gravity of the situation at hand. While my mother and sister were at the hospital and I at home, I found myself listening to music, playing the piano, gaming on my Playstation, watching television…further down the line, after Dad was transferred to Rashid, I was even able to catch a touring show of the Broadway musical, *Hairspray*, in Dubai. My ability to do these things confused me, so much in fact, that one day, I actually sat my mother down and talked about this. Mind you, I was sixteen.

"Mom, do I love Dad?"

Her eyebrows came together in confusion.

"What?" she asked perplexed, almost amused.

"Everyone else seems so worried all the time, and while you and Nasha are off pacing up and down in the hospital, I'm comfortably sitting at home watching TV, playing music or whatever."

"OK…?"

"I just don't feel as worried as everyone else is, you know? It's like I'm calmer, like I can do all these things as if nothing's wrong. Is this some sort of indication that I love Dad any less than you guys? Doesn't that make me kinda heartless?"

My mother laughed and hugged me. While my calmness made me feel ashamed of myself, her reaction puzzled me.

"My darling, please don't stop doing anything you're doing. The fact that you can still do all these things, that you can remain calm right now is your greatest asset. You need to continue living life as normally as possible. Worrying will get you nowhere, and will only cause more heartache and stress for you."

At first, I wasn't convinced by her answer, and I think it showed. Much to my annoyance, my apparent innocence and naivety still gave her reason to laugh.

"Tell you what honey- let me do the worrying, why don't you provide the calmness for the family? We'll all need it sooner or later."

"Has it occurred to you that I don't think this is funny?"

Mom hugged me again, tighter than ever.

"Sweetheart, I'm dead serious. You need to be as calm as possible. We all do. And to answer your question, my love, you love your father very much. And you bet your bottom dollar he loves you too. Don't ever forget that."

It took a while, but her words finally did make sense to me, and I realized how right she was. It was necessary to remain calm in this situation, and do whatever I could to keep myself distracted to a certain extent. I found this especially true for the events that transpired after his move to Rashid Hospital.

CHAPTER 8

SATAN STRIKES BACK

After what seemed like hours, the doctors were finally done examining me, and I was wheeled out on the stretcher.

Where the Hell are they taking me now?

Operating room? ICU? And where in Heaven's name is my family?

My mind was once again running at breakneck speed, and I developed this sinking feeling that all was not well. I was losing whatever little control I felt I had of myself. The pain started to drift away as my body became completely numb. I realized that so much as moving a finger, or batting an eyelid was becoming effortful.

What's happening? Pervaiz, why can't you feel any pain? Is someone or something else controlling you? Don't let that happen! Stay conscious, for God's sake stay conscious!

I hoped and prayed with all my might that this was not another out-of-body experience.

Has God changed his mind? Is He pulling me up? I don't bloody well think so! God, if you want a rematch just because you couldn't stand being checkmated once, so be it!

But no matter how I argued, I could feel God winning already. The pain was fearfully low, and was decreasing with each passing second. Ironically, it didn't comfort me- I'd rather have been in pain if it meant retaining control of my body and senses. The drugs started to take effect, as I realized I could hardly move, and my senses were shutting down. My vision was reduced to a blurry haze, and sounds around me were nothing more than incoherent, incomprehensible murmurs. My only consolation, for now at least, was that I could still feel the stretcher under me.

Alright Pervaiz, stressing out is clearly not helping anyone. Just chill out and try to keep focused. Hopefully this will soon pass.

How I wished that was the case. As time passed, as the pain reduced to a bare minimum,

I began to lose track of everything…the date, time, where I was- all the facts started to get muddled. My mind was able to recollect scenes, not stories.

Vans… policemen…hospitals…am I having some sort of memory lapse…?

By now, my body was completely devoid of all pain. But something didn't seem right. Both my eyes were closed, I knew that, and yet, I could see. And things were no longer fuzzy- my vision was better than it had ever been! I anxiously looked around and about me, and concluded that I was in a hospital. Stranger than that, I was alone.

Where are all the other patients? I can't possibly be the only one! Where is Maz? Ah, she must be stuck in traffic…yeah…that's it! Dear God, please let Nasha be with her- Lord knows Maz is, at the very least, directionally challenged.

I examined my surroundings a little more closely. My room wasn't all that bad, in fact, it was rather pleasant. It was lovely and spacious, for starters, and well decorated. A beautiful blue, with images of clouds and cherubim decked the walls. It was like staring at a painting by one of the masters. Above me, a gorgeous chandelier sparkled, filling the room with its beams of gold. And best of all, the room had a window to a luscious, green and well-kept garden. The flower beds were overflowing with red and white roses, and massive animal hedges of the most intricate design occupied the surrounding area. A beautifully carved stone fountain, whose water shot out of it like a hot spring, was placed in the center of the garden. The beauty was simply indescribable.

What kind of hospital is this? It seems more like a hotel. And is this in Sharjah, or have they brought me to Dubai? Damn it, where am I?!

Just then, I heard the door opening, and my heart leaped with joy.

Well, it's about time Maz and Nasha arrived. I hope Ardavan isn't with them- I don't want him to see me like this. Wait, who the Hell is this?

A figure, dressed in a green surgical outfit, walked in the room. A mask covered its face, and a hair net its head. Its hands wore latex gloves, and pushed a cart on which a black bag rested. I beckoned it closer, but it ignored me, and proceeded to empty the contents of its bag on the sliding table across my bed. I watched in awe and wonder- the objects were bigger than the bag itself!

How on Earth did it fit all these things in that tiny carrier? Are the headlines tomorrow going to read "Mary Poppins Loses Signature Carpet Bag"?

Finally, the figure approached me and ripped the mask off its face. My jaw dropped.

"MEHER?"

Sure enough, it was Meher, an old friend I met way back in college. She beamed at me, waving her hand in greeting.

"Hi Pervaiz!" she quipped cheerfully.

"What in Heaven's name are you doing here? And what's with the surgeon's outfit? I asked.

She simply smiled and said "What do you mean, 'What am I doing here?' Pervaiz? The moment I heard you'd had an accident, I rushed over."

"Very sweet of you to visit me. Thank you," I said smiling. But Meher had something more to say.

"Haha, this is more than a friendly visit, Pervaiz. I'm here to operate on you."

Completely taken aback, at first I thought I hadn't heard correctly. This had to be my senses fading away again.

"Come again? Did you just say you're here to *operate* on me?" I uttered in absolute disbelief.

"Yes, Pervaiz," said Meher, a hint of annoyance in her voice, as if I had insulted her intelligence. "I'm a qualified surgeon."

The more the conversation progressed, the more ludicrous the whole scenario sounded.

"And just when the Hell did you become a doctor? And how did you get here so fast? My own family's not here yet!"

"Oh, I was in the middle of a medical conference in Dubai, and was informed that you were critical, and needed urgent medical attention. I dropped everything and headed straight to you," came a matter-of-fact reply.

Something was amiss. None of this made any sense, and the whole thing was too bizarre to be real. I had to have been losing my mind; this could not *possibly* be actually happening. It just couldn't. But no matter how I tried to rationalize the situation, this was one puzzle I just could not piece together.

"Meher, are you serious?" I tried again, desperately.

"Yes, Pervaiz, I'm very serious!" she exclaimed, now completely affronted. "Your liver is in really bad shape, and needs to be replaced instantly. If I don't remove it right now, it will lead to poisoning, resulting in certain death. Now, is this in any way unclear, or may I proceed?

"Mother of Christ, Meher, wait a minute!" I yelled. "If you remove my liver, what are you going to replace it with?"

"Oh, right," she said, snapping her fingers. I almost forgot, you'll be needing this. It's your liver replacement."

She turned towards her toolkit and pulled out what looked remotely like a mud-coated, brown tennis ball that had been hit by Roger Federer's racquet a few times too many.

"What the fuck is that?" I screamed in protest, pointing to the ball of dung staring back at me.

"It's an artificial liver, of course," said Meher, growing more and more impatient. "I'm sorry it doesn't look like a bar of gold," she added, sarcasm oozing from her every vein.

"Meher, this is completely insane. You can't possibly-"

"Pervaiz, you do not have any more time to waste. Stop arguing!" Meher said sternly, like a mother trying to discipline a five year old. "Now, let me do my job."

"LET YOU DO YOUR JOB??? HAVE YOU LOST YOUR FUCKING MIND??? GET ME MAZ RIGHT NOW!!!"

"She's in the waiting room, Pervaiz," she said calmly, although she made no attempt to hide her disgust at my tantrums. "Don't worry, I'll be done in about forty-five minutes."

And then, as if by invisible straps, I felt myself being tied down to the bed. Something or someone was holding me in place. Smiling, she turned back towards her bag, rummaging through it. My breathing became fast and shallow as I started panicking. *What the Hell is going on?*

"Meher, please just listen to me," I pleaded, trying my level best to reason with her. "You haven't looked at my files, my X-rays, tests…you can't just show up out of the blues and replace my liver. I haven't spoken to any anesthesiologist, no one's briefed me on the surg-"

"Aha! Here it is!" she exclaimed triumphantly. With glee, she turned towards me. The steel blade shone against the light of the chandelier, and the hilt glistened in her hands…it was my replica of the Excalibur, the legendary sword of King Arthur, one of the crowning jewels of my collection.

"Damn it, Meher, that's mine! Where did you get it?"

Suddenly, it hit me, an awful realization that brought a lump to my throat. "Meher, please don't tell me that's what you're planning on operating with," I whispered at a stratospheric octave.

"Now, just hold still, Pervaiz. This won't hurt a bit," she said, grinning devilishly through her teeth as she approached the side of the bed. At this point, I couldn't tell who was more insane, me or her. My efforts to break the invisible bonds that bound me to the bed were in vain. I struggled, pushed, pulled, screamed, shook with all my might as if emulating a violent seizure, but it was all for nothing. In a panic, my eyes fell upon hers, and caught an unmistakable demonic twinkle in them. A maniacal smile spread across her face as she raised the sword above her head, the blade aimed right above my chest.

"Meher, wait…NO!"

The pain was excruciating beyond measure, and my screams could have shattered the chandelier above us. Meher had driven the sword so far through me, I could actually feel the blade against my vertebrae. Blood gushed out of me like a hot spring, splattering everywhere- the walls, the ceiling, Meher's clothes, my face… the walls, which were blue just seconds ago were now streaked with red. Blood trickled down the faces of the cherubim like tears, as if they wept for me, or they could feel my pain themselves. But Meher was far from done. Grasping the hilt firmly in her hands, like a fishmonger gutting a shark, she dragged the blade lengthwise across my torso until my naval, ripping my chest in half right down the middle.

"AAAAARRRRGGGGHHHH!!!!"

The pain would surely drive me to insanity, if I had not already reached that point by then, I thought. Meher took no notice of my agonizing screams, and continued to tear through my body. I begged, pleaded inside my head for this ordeal to be nothing more than a nightmare; that I could close and reopen my eyes, and none of this would be real. But God damn it- how does one close eyes that are already shut? And how in Heaven's name do closed eyes see anything? I had to somehow come to terms with the fact that this was not a dream, that my situation was very real.

"Gotcha!" Meher exclaimed victoriously. Excitedly, she took off her surgical gloves, and shoved her arm all the way up to her elbow through my abdomen, working her way up. With one firm tug, she ripped out a pale green, flabby mass covered in blood and other body fluids.

"Here you are," she said joyfully, presenting me with the mass, like a deranged Santa Claus.

Before I could utter a word, she hurled my liver across the room, saying, "You won't be needing that anymore!"

SPLAT!

The organ landed on the wall and stuck itself in place.

"See Pervaiz? All done," she said, while removing her surgeon gear. "Now just relax, and I'll tell the nurses to come and stitch you up." Surprisingly, she didn't need to project much to make herself heard over my screams.

With that, she sauntered out of the room with her bag, leaving me drenched in a pool of my own blood, sweat and tears. She didn't pack the Excalibur for some reason, but I was grateful she left it behind. It was lying right next to me on the bed, and I so desperately wanted to pick it up and slit my own throat. I could end it all, this whole episode, the pain, the misery...I just needed to lift it up and bring it to my neck, but alas, the blade seemed to weigh a ton. In fact, moving was proving to be more and more difficult. It was if I had exhausted all my energy trying to break free from the bed before being mutilated by a quack.

Death was imminent, I was sure of it. How could anyone possibly survive such an extraordinary loss of blood? How could anyone live through the pain, which made seconds feel like hours? Still screaming, I felt my lungs would collapse any second, but how could I stop?

God, if I am to die, grant me one last wish- whatever happens, just please don't let my family see me like this.

The hands of the wall clock pointed at five, whether in the morning or evening, it didn't specify.

Wait a minute, where did that clock come from? That wasn't there a second ago.

I strained my neck, turning it towards the window, which was somehow open. It was dark outside- had the sun not yet risen, or had it already set while Meher was playing real-life 'Operation'?

Just then, a jet of bluish-green darted through the window, landing on my chest. I was greeted by the most stunning bird I had ever laid eyes upon. A gorgeous combination of neon blue and jade green, its beauty was breathtaking. For a split second, I forgot how much pain I was in as I marveled at its prettiness.

"I swear, if you start building a nest in me…" I knew it sounded stupid, but after everything that happened so far, I figured anything was possible. But the bird didn't proceed to fill my insides with twigs and leaves. It cooed at me, flapped its wings and flew over to the table beside me, from which it picked up a tiny needle in its beak. It flew back to my chest, and, as if trained by the world's top surgeons, began to stitch my wounds back together.

I was silenced into awe. I couldn't believe what was happening. A bird, a tiny bird no bigger than my palm, proved to be a lifesaver. A realization that escaped me was that with each completed stitch, the pain decreased. Moreover, my body, as if through some mystic channel of energy, regained its ability to move. I could blink, move my arms…It dexterously completed stitching me up, while I sat back and watched in wonder. Within seconds, the bird was done, and my pain was no more.

I stared at the winged creature in shock and disbelief. It cooed once more, as if to say, "It was nothing." I anxiously examined my body, and was met with the strangest sight. My gashes, the blood...everything was gone. That bird did not only stop the pain and stitch me back up, it cleaned me up too. There was not a scar on my body, and not a drop of blood on my chest. I anxiously reached for my face- it was completely dry. I looked around myself- the walls had regained that pretty shade of blue, and the cherubim eyes were no longer bawling out bloody tears.

What does one say to a bird that just saved one from relentless agony? "Thank you"? Even if I did, the words sounded insufficient. Even though I was too stunned to speak, I'm sure my feathered friend knew I was grateful. It flew back to the window sill, turned her head towards me, and chirped cheerfully before finally taking off into the darkness. Fascinated, but still speechless on the bed, with only my confusion for a companion, I was left to ponder over the events that just occurred; whether I was dreaming or deluded, awake or asleep, alive or dead.

Grinning from ear to ear, I ran my hands across my chest, just to make sure that all my wounds were healed, and this had not all been my imagination running wild with me. There were no slits, cuts, bruises, or stitches…my body had completely healed. I reached for my Excalibur, but it was gone. I wonder if the bird knew what I wanted to do with it, and thought it meaningless that it should remain with me now.

God, you really know how to scare the pants off someone.

Chuckling at that final thought, I turned over, closed my eyes, and thought no more. My only wish was for the remainder of my sleep to be peaceful, uneventful and uninterrupted…

Lord knows if I actually did get some sleep or not, but if I did, it felt like just about fifteen seconds. A knock on the door woke me up, much to my annoyance.

I don't care who you jokers are. Unless you're family, leave me the Hell alone.

Two men walked into the room. At first, I thought my eyes were playing tricks on me. They were dressed in dapper black suits, and sported perfectly polished black shoes. They approached me, and each gave me a firm, vice-like grip of a handshake, to which I reciprocated with my mouth open, completely aghast. They then took their seats on either edge of my bed. I got more than I bargained for; these two gentlemen were not family, but nor were they strangers or friends. They were, well, me.

Pervaiz, it's official; you're finally completely off your rocker. A hundred and one percent loony, no doubt of it.

I didn't know if I should laugh, call for help, or strangle the apparitions and go back to bed.

You weren't happy with one of me were you, God? Had to go and make three of us...what were you thinking??

"So three simple questions for you guys," I said, staring at the Pervaizs across from me.

"Who are you, what do you want, and why the bloody fuck do you look like me?"

"Well, it's like this Pervaiz," started one of the apparitions, in my voice, which didn't surprise me. If they looked like me, why shouldn't they have sounded like me? "Maz has sent us to inform you that-"

"I *beg* your pardon!" I exclaimed, cutting him off midsentence. "*Maz* sent you two?"

"She wants us to tell you that you have broken twenty-eight bones, you have developed septicemia, and your liver, lungs and kidneys have all gone for a toss," continued the other, disregarding my rudeness. "Oh, and that your chances of survival are next to nil," it concluded.

"To cut a long story short, you're no longer useful to her in this condition. So we're here to, how should we say this...*recycle* you...? If you survive the process, Nasha *may* take you back as her Dad. Maz is still in two minds about that, but we can't say for sure what Ardavan says about the whole affair since he's not here yet."

The longest and loudest silence I've ever experienced ensued. My face resembled that of a kindergartener who was just explained trigonometric calculus by his teacher. The narrow food table was right next to me, and I was tempted beyond measure to pick it up and hammer the stupid clean out of Laurel and Hardy. So Meher was right- my liver *had* deteriorated to uselessness. Were these two jokers right about my lungs and kidneys? But I had no time to ponder over the situation, or recover from the shock. Before I knew it, I was lifted up by the two Pervaizs like a rag doll, and rammed into the wall, head first.

If there was one thing I learned to appreciate at that moment, it was how incredible the human body actually is. So meticulously and intricately designed, it is far from fragile. It really is stunning, what the body can endure without finally succumbing to death. Screaming in agony, clutching my cranium, it felt as if more than a hundred bones in my body were breaking, that the blow to my head had sent a shockwave through the rest of my system, destroying anything and everything in its path. How I wished the blow cracked my skull, or at the very least, knocked me out. But I was at the mercy of the apparitions, which controlled what I could feel, whether I lived or died.

But that wasn't enough fun for the demonic duo. To my horror, my eyes darted towards a machine that had appeared in the middle of the room. It was an automated stone crusher- a massive, bulky, towering object was staring back at me. My apparitions gave me no time to scream in fear or protest. My head still in my hands, they seized me and shoved me into the opening of the machine, attempting to have me crushed alive.

The noise from the crushing process created such a din, I could barely hear myself scream. The weight and force against my body, I felt, matched that of a herd of wild elephants practicing the foxtrot on me. Each bone in my body let out a blood-curdling shriek, one that could have put Lucille La Verne's famous Disney movie screams to shame. Simultaneously, I could feel my flesh was turning into pulp, as if I were a piece of fruit being run through a juicer.

Yelling, begging non-stop for relief, I emerged from the machine feeling flatter than a doormat. The two Pervaizs took no notice of my pain, but grabbed my legs, and flung me back on the bed. They began to examine me, scratching their chins, heads, conversing with each other in a very business-like manner, as if they were evaluating my profitability as a financial undertaking. They murmured to each other indistinctively, but I could make out phrases- something about 'not being good enough' and 'too few returns'.

One of them picked me up again, and headed towards the window.

"He's useless," he said to the other. With that, he tossed me out like a garbage bag.

I was falling at breakneck speed, and the rush of adrenalin was unparalleled. I felt my body painfully contort itself back into its normal, bulky figure while in midair. I snapped my eyes shut, bracing myself for the impact on the ground.

WHAP!

I landed, but this was nowhere near hard enough to be the ground; in fact, the surface was rather soft and downy, like a pillow. I slowly opened my eyes, and saw that I was on a large cushion. The pain had completely disappeared again, and I was unscathed. By now I was used to the bizarre way it would come and go as it pleased, as if it had a mind of its own. Getting up to inspect my surroundings more closely, I noticed I was surrounded by walls of sticks and twigs. Looking at the cushion underneath me, I saw feathers of familiar blue and green scattered around. Where had I seen these colors before? And then it struck me- that bird, that blue and green bird that stitched me up after Meher had her way with me- this must be its nest! Excitedly, I spun around, hoping to meet my savior a second time, and was greeted with a rather 'big' surprise.

There, standing before me, was the bird, except it was no longer a tiny, scrawny little thing. In fact, that was now me. The creature had grown to the size of the largest pachyderm.

"Damn, Tweetie, what happened to you?" I asked, chuckling at my cheek. Tweetie, on the other hand, did not look amused. It glared at me, like a mother at her child, who just spilled a jug of milk across the kitchen table. Something bad was about to happen, I could sense that much. Had I insulted the bird with my cartoon reference? Before I could answer that though, the bird bent down, picked me up in its beak, and proceeded to take me to the edge of the nest.

"Hey, hey, hey you twit! Put me down before you drop me!" I yelled in a panic.

Frantically, my eyes searched for a way to break free from the bird's grip, but I couldn't budge. They fell upon what was waiting for me at the end of the drop. There, stories below me, I could see my two doppelgangers at my bed, beckoning, encouraging the bird to release me.

"Oh God, no! Please- I'll just hail a cab and go home!" I pleaded, but the bird disregarded my cries for mercy, and opened its beak.

"AAAAAAAHHHHHH!!!!!!"

THUMP!

Within seconds of a freefall, I found myself back in the hospital ward, flopped down on my bed. Panicking, confused, I quickly glanced around to see what had become of my two shadow selves, but they were nowhere to be found. I sighed a breath of relief. I had absolutely no idea where they were, and I had absolutely no wish to know. They were gone, and that was all that mattered.

Moments later, I felt something slithering over my right shoulder like a snake. Reaching for my shoulder, what my hand grabbed made me want to kiss Satan himself. It was a nurse-call cord! Without wasting another microsecond, I pushed the button. Maybe one of the nurses could explain what was going on, or at the very least, get Laurel and Hardy off my back. The door opened, and in came a figure in blue scrubs, a white hairnet and face mask, and white sneakers. A stethoscope hung around its neck like a medal of honor, and it carried a clipboard at its side. Beaming, I called the nurse towards me. As the figure approached, it started to remove its face mask and hair net. My smile instantly vanished, and was replaced with a weary, frustrated grim look that hardly suited me.

"Dear God, why? *WHY*?"

It was Laurel. Or Hardy, whichever. I could have cried.

"You called for me, sir?" inquired my double, in an Alfred Pennyworth manner.

"Yes I did. Do u have a baseball bat?" I asked, with all the sarcasm I could muster.

"Why would you need a baseball bat?

"BECAUSE, YOU MOTHERFUCKING SON OF A BITCH, I WANT TO SHOVE IT SO FAR UP YOUR ASS THAT IT COMES OUT OF YOUR GOD-FORESAKEN MOUTH!" I yelled, spit strewing on him.

"That could prove quite deadly, sir," my doppelganger quipped in his mocking butler voice. "Why do you seek to kill me this way, when I'm here to give you a new pair of legs?"

"What?" I whispered, frustrated and bemused.

"Yes, sir. Your legs can no longer support your weight. Here I come, providing a solution to your dilemma, and you express a desire to push a baseball bat up my rectum? Tsk tsk."

His corny accent continued to annoy me, but that was the least of my concerns. I noticed that he carried the same bag that Meher brought in with her before slicing me open. Nurse Pervaiz opened up the bag and pulled out a massive, battery-powered chainsaw.

"WHAT THE BLOODY FUCK ARE YOU DOING WITH THAT?" I demanded, although I was sure I knew what was coming.

"Quiet, Pervaiz!" snapped the phantom. "And don't squirm, or I might mess this up." Before I could open my mouth in protest, he pulled on the engine cord, placed the blade over my legs, right above my knees, and proceeded to lower the saw until it made contact with my flesh.

Blood and fragments of my bones flew in all directions. Within seconds, both my legs were sawed clean off, and lay at the foot of my bed. My agonizing screams filled the room, and the apparition completely overlooked my pain and pleas for mercy.

"KILL ME! *KILL ME!*" I repeated, but my cries fell upon deaf ears. To put an end to my life would have been humane, and he seemed to be devoid of all humanity. But he wasn't done with me yet. My double headed back towards his bag and pulled out a china plate, a silver fork and knife and a white napkin. He came back to my bed, sat himself down, and I watched in horror as he started to cut my legs into small cubes and devour them, like they were some cannibalistic delicacy. It was a gruesome sight.

My screams of pain evolved into shrieks of terror, and I wanted nothing more than to be able to pull my own eyes out of their sockets. With this, I had had enough. I didn't know whether I was simply a victim in a nightmarish fantasy, or I had gone completely insane, or all this was really happening to me, but I didn't care. It had to end, and it had to end now. I made a grab for the chainsaw, but my double, who knew exactly what I wanted to do with it, snatched it away from me and dangled it scornfully above my head with one hand, while continually munching away at my legs with the other. Trying to grab a hold of it, I was like a dog, pitifully begging its master for a treat. I could feel a mixture of sweat and tears of pain, anger and frustration roll down my face, and into my open, screaming mouth.

Just when I thought I was doomed to spend an eternity in this nightmare, I heard the unmistakable cry of an eagle. In desperation, I looked to where the sound came from. There, on the window sill, was perched a bald American eagle, majestic, beautiful, mighty and powerful. Swiftly and gracefully, it swooped in and came face to face with my doppelganger. It spread its wings to their full span, flapping them in his face, and pecked away at his head while its razor-sharp talons made a grab for the remainder of my legs. Terrified, the apparition fled the room like a startled sheep.

Screeching in triumph, the brazen eagle perched itself upon my chest. I expected its weight to be far beyond what my body could take at this point, but it surprisingly felt lighter than one of its feathers. It brought its face up to mine, and my eyes fell upon what it was carrying in its beak- a small, shiny but sharp needle. At that moment, I knew exactly what it was here for. Like the bluebird before it, the eagle, with meticulous care and strategy, began reassembling my legs, and stitching them back together as if they were torn garments. Not only did I have to admire its craftsmanship, but the entire procedure was absolutely painless, which was more than I could ask for at this point.

With each stitch, the stains of blood vanished, and like before, the room, my clothes, the bed, the walls were all spotless by the time the eagle was done. I wondered why it wasn't the bluebird that revisited me to mend my wounds. Perhaps the situation was a little more drastic, and called for a slightly more experienced beak. Once I was fully stitched up, the gorgeous creature stretched a wing to half its span, and started to gently caress my legs, like a mother caressing her child's scabs in an attempt to heal them. Its feathers were softer than the downiest pillow in the world. Finally, after resting its body against mine for five minutes, it looked at me one last time, gave a final screech, and took off out of the window from which it came, leaving me to thoroughly process what just transpired.

So in one night, or day, whatever it was, I was mutilated, crushed, flattened, flung, dropped and eaten alive by a lookalike of myself. Yet, I came out of it alive, and very much in my mind. My ultimately saving graces were two angels that visited me in bird form. Satan was once again foiled, and in some far off place, I knew he was shaking his fists in fury.

What a day! Apart from how exhausted and drained of energy I was, that was the only thing that my mind could think. At that moment, I made a promise to myself that I would get as much sleep as I could.

Meher, strange apparitions, even God Himself, could knock on the door of your ward, Pervaiz, you will not stir, whether they want to inform you of developments in your condition, or that the sky is falling, or of the latest English Royal Family scandal.

CHAPTER 9

STRANGE AND STRANGER BEDFELLOWS

Sleep would be comforting only as long as it lasted me. I'd have to wake up sooner or later, and I would still be disoriented. I had no knowledge of time or date.

What's causing this to happen? Why do I still have such harrowing, dreadful visions, whether my eyes are open or closed? What if I were to pretend nothing was amiss...just let events and nightmares unfold as they'd come...how long could it possibly last?

But no matter what I'd do, the madness still raged on, and I was unable to put my finger on the source of the trouble. Something somewhere had gone horribly wrong, and just how long it was before things finally started to look up is not something I remember...

Movement...I could feel it, but it was not my stretcher, for the surface I lay on was perfectly still. I was not being wheeled away. The ride had a few bumps in it, but was smooth overall. I was in a vehicle, being driven somewhere... My left hand would repeatedly fall off the stretcher, and someone would keep on placing it back. Groggily, I opened my eyes, hoping what I would see would not be another fragment of my imagination. I caught a glimpse of my boss's wife, Dr. Hina Mirza. She stayed with me all throughout the ride, wherever I was being taken. I was informed only later on that I was being transferred from Qassimi to Rashid Hospital in Dubai...

*

I saw her, standing at the edge of my bed, tucking in the sheets...there was my beloved wife. She smiled at me, and I smiled back. How beautiful she looked, and how elated I was to see her again, even if she was just another apparition. She came towards me, beaming brighter than the sun, and flung her arms around me. I couldn't narrate how much I missed her warm embrace… so loving, so tender, so…*lifelike*…in fact, if this was an apparition, I wanted nothing more than for it to last forever. But her touch, her scent, the feel of her body against mine…it all seemed so realistic…hoping against hope, I took a chance…I simply had to ask…

Owing to the tracheostomy, in a hoarse whisper I said to her "Maz…? Is that you? Is that really you?"

"Yes, sweetheart, who else do you want it to be?" came the reply, in a gentle, slightly confused tone.

I could have cried. How I wished the hands of time would freeze so I could cherish my bittersweet reencounter with my wife for eternity. After much affirmation, she assured me that this was no vision, and that she was very much in the hospital ward with me. It was then that I realized that the world I was currently in was very much real, and not another of my wild fantasies. Maz's face lit up as she repeatedly kissed my lips and forehead. She then placed her head on my chest, while I held her in tightly, determined to never let go.

But the events that transpired just days, maybe even hours ago…Meher, my two shadow selves, the birds…

"Maz, where are my legs?" I asked urgently. By the look on her face, my wife was clearly bemused.

"Your legs? Right where they should be, honey. Why?"

"Please show them to me. Let me see them!"

"But sweetheart, can't you feel your own legs?"

"Maz, *please*!"

She surely must have thought I had lost my senses completely. As it is I had to rely now on them lip reading me as not a whisper could I emit any longer. Nevertheless, she was obliging to my strange requests. She proceeded towards the edge of the bed, pulled back the sheets, grasped my ankles, and lifted both my legs high for me to see. Sure enough, they were both there, completely intact. Not so much as a hair was missing. I sighed a breath of relief, and felt the color return to my cheeks.

"So what the Hell was that jackass eating?" I demanded.

"Darling, what on Earth are you talking about?" asked Maz, now completely and utterly perplexed. "What was who eating?"

For a moment, I looked as confused as she was. It was a few seconds later that I realized that everything- the mad surgeon, the Pervaiz phantoms, the bluebird, the eagle…none of that could have been real. Dismissing the entire conversation, I beckoned my wife near to me again, kissed her forehead and firmly gripped her hands in mine. There they remained, for what seemed like forever, before…

I found myself in a small, dimly lit closet of a room. Surrounding me were tiny, rapidly blinking bulbs emitting a variety of red, blue and green, and dozens of switches and levers. Large, complex-looking dials displaying an array of alphanumeric codes stared back at me from a control panel. Large, black revolving armchairs backed me, and strange noises occasionally broke the silence- sounds of laser beams shooting out of their guns, automatic doors sliding open and close…it looked like a small, highly advanced pilot's cockpit.

I tried to climb out of bed to inspect the premises more closely, but as before, I was glued to my sheets.

Oh, dear God, not again…

A small window was just a few feet away from me. Craning my neck, I struggled to see what was outside. Clouds- one fluffy ball of white cotton after another passed me by…in dismay, I flopped my head back down into my pillow.

Damn it, where are they taking me now?

Suddenly, my eyes fell upon a figure in a blue uniform standing next to me. He looked sternly ahead, as if mesmerized by the flashes of red, blue and green.

"Who are you, and where the Hell am I?" I demanded.

Without shifting his gaze, the space cadet said to me, "We have been told to take you to Planet Vulcan. Captain James Kirk and First Officer Mr. Spock would like a word with you."

OK, back the USS Enterprise up a second. Why on Earth is he telling me that the leading characters from my favorite Sci-fi franchise are looking to talk with me? Where am I, and where is Maz? She was with me not a minute ago! And why the bloody fuck can't I get out of bed??

Completely annoyed by all these crazy shenanigans, and by the fact that something was pinning me down, I turned my head back toward the cadet, determined to get answers. But before I could open my mouth, he smiled at me, winked, and vanished without a trace…

*

I distinctly remember this one day when I slept like a baby in his mother's arms, with no visits from birds, mad surgeons, doppelgangers or spacemen. It was absolute bliss, and I woke up feeling better than I had felt for what seemed like years. I could feel all my body parts, knew exactly where I was, felt in complete control of myself and my senses. I told Maz about my peaceful and relaxing sleep, and she beamed at me.

"I wonder if that means it's working…," she murmured.

I was slightly taken aback. "What's working? What drug did they put me on?"

"No drug, sweetheart. There's something you need to know."

"OK…"

"While you were asleep, a woman we've never met before came to see you, really just out of the goodness of her heart."

"Who?" I asked, puzzled. To help a stranger in need on the street is one thing, but to visit a stranger in hospital is something else altogether. "And how did she know about me?"

"Her name is Goolcher Navdar. Darayus brought her here."

"Darayus…our priest, Darayus? You mean she's Parsi?"

"Yes. He performs the ceremonies at her place too. Anyway, while she was here, she performed *reiki* on-"

"I'm sorry- she performed *what*?" I murmured, cutting her off.

"*Reiki*," she continued, "is some Chinese-Japanese healing technique. She basically channeled energy into you through touch. It apparently activates the body's natural healing mechanism, and helps restore physical and emotional well-being."

I laughed bemused. "So let me get this straight- you let a witch doctor into the room, and she performed some voodoo crap on me?" I asked, chuckling.

"Darling," Maz said, in a slightly reprimanding tone, "don't be mean. She is not a witch-doctor, and there was no voodoo going on. If anything, whatever she did seems to have helped you."

"Oh, it has, for sure. Compared to what I've been through, Maz, I feel like nine hundred and ninety-nine thousand, nine hundred and ninety-nine bucks right now."

Maz looked at me, her lips contorting into a smirk. "What's with being a dollar short of a million?"

"Let's take it one step at a time."

*

A nurse was fidgeting with some machines and monitors beside my bed. I had to be sure.

"Where am I?" I asked her.

She looked at me, smiled, and said, "You are in the Rashid Hospital sir, in the ICU ward."

"When did I get back from Vulcan?"

"Sorry?"

"Never mind," I said, having gathered all the affirmation that I was in the real world as I needed. "What are these machines around me?"

"Well as a result of your liver failure back in Qassimi, we've had to begin dialysis."

Maz sighed, but I had a more pressing issue to address.

"Nurse, my ribs and back are killing me. Why is that?"

"Sir, you have multiple fractures all over, so that pain is expected. But don't worry, I'll soon put you to sleep."

And like a five year old having heard the dreaded "s" word, I threw a tantrum.

"Not a chance in Hell! *Sleep?* I just woke up after ages, and you want me to go back to *sleep*?"

"Sir, I have to follow the doctor's orders," she said, completely taken aback by my apparent immaturity.

"Forget the orders! Get me the doctor!" I exclaimed. She walked out, giving me a look of complete perplexity and disgust. I could have sworn I heard her 'tsk' under her breath as she approached the door.

"Sweetheart, please control yourself. What do you want with the doctor?" asked Maz, who witnessed my little outburst.

"Don't worry, Maz. I just want to ask him a couple of questions."

A while later, the doctor, whose name unfortunately escapes me, walked in, and I ensured that minimal time was wasted on the meet and greet. I told him to pull up a chair, because I needed his undivided attention. He was clearly amused by my peculiar request, but obliged nonetheless, and that's all I could ask for.

He patiently sat through a detailed recount of my experiences with Meher, the birds, the apparitions, and the Star Trek special. I'm sure he tried stifling a laugh every now and then, but I couldn't care less. Most of the stories clearly had my wife disturbed.

Finally, when I had relived the last of the episodes, I said, "Doc, please, I need the entire honest truth. What's wrong with me? Where did all these visions come from?"

"It's not your fault, my friend," came a gentle and sympathetic reply. "Nothing is wrong with you, well, mentally anyway, you are not going insane, and never were. What you were experiencing was the unfortunate side effect of morphine. We have been injecting you with this drug just to keep you pain-free."

"Pain-free my ass," I muttered under my breath, although judging by Maz's stern expression, it was not as quiet as I'd imagined it to be, not that I gave a hoot. "Doc, you have no clue about the pain I've gone through!"

"I'm very well aware of it, Pervaiz," he calmly said to me. "As I said, this is an unfortunate side-effect of the drug. It's a hard narcotic made from opium, and hospitals are just about the only places licensed to administer it for pain-control. It doesn't surprise me that you've been hallucinating. And the horror you've experienced, while not hoped for, is not unheard of. You might have issues with memory, be unable to recognize people or places, or see, hear or feel things that are not there."

I lay there, trying to take in a tidal wave of information. So the quack surgeon, the bird healers, the doppelgangers, the *Enterprise*...they were all hallucinations brought about by a drug?!

"OK, Doc," I said to him, determinedly. "Enough is enough. I don't want any more of this shit pumped into me. Is that clear?"

Slightly affronted, but tickled nonetheless, the doctor replied, "My friend you have no idea what you are saying. You will unleash Hell upon yourself if you refuse morphine. An hour from now, the pain will blow you out of your mind."

"I'm sorry to contradict you, but it's you who has no idea of what you are saying. I'll take my chances with the pain- I'm accustomed to it by now. Report me to the chief medical officer for all I care, but I will not take another drop of this drug. Period."

I undoubtedly instilled the fear of God into him, because he realized I meant business.

"OK, let's do this: we'll reduce the dosage; it should be concentrated enough to manage the pain, but not potent enough to be able to make you hallucinate so horrifically. But you must understand that we'll be playing this by ear; if we feel at any given point in time that the pain level is beyond your control, we will have no choice but to restart the original dosage."

Without a second's hesitation, I shook on our new pact. I chose to live through the pain than live through one waking nightmare after the other.

Just days later though, a new problem arose. Maz noticed that over time, my skin was beginning to adopt a pale yellow pigmentation. She immediately inquired as to what this was, and the doctor then informed her that the severity of the state of my kidneys had led to jaundice.

"How dangerous is it?"

"Jaundice isn't really a disease as much as it is a side effect of the underlying issue, which is the kidney failure. It's more of an indication of the severity of his kidneys' condition. So if his kidneys begin to heal, the yellow will disappear. All we can do is hope for the best."

He was right- that was really all we could do. I must say, it's in times like these when one can really experience the healing power of prayer. My friends and family around me, and even the doctors and nurses assured me I was kept in their daily prayers. With the passage of time, I realized I was back to my usual five-year-old shenanigans. I'd fiddle with machines and monitors I wasn't supposed to, *accidentally* press the "call nurse" button on my bed railing, and flick through the TV channels until either 'Tom and Jerry' or 'Looney Toons' appeared on the screen. Better than that, I slept well, usually dreamlessly. I'd wake up in the morning, greet doctors and nurses (Dr. Baqer Ali would visit me on a daily basis, enquiring as to how I was holding up), and interact with family and friends who came to visit. And best of all, I regained full control of my mind, body and senses. The feeling of triumph was unparalleled. At long last, I was able to fulfil my ardent wish of telling my family not to worry; that come hail, Hell or high waters, all, in time, would be back to normal.

There was, however, one pastime that caught my fancy more than anything else, at least, for the first few days that I was spared from the nightmarish visions I initially endured. I was curious to know more about morphine, the apparent miracle drug, which was supposedly so effective in relieving pain that its benefits are thought to outweigh the drawbacks of hallucinations. The scientific jargon was unable to hold my interest for long, and besides, the doctor had already briefed me enough on it. My research took me to the fascinating realm of Greek Mythology. Morpheus was thought to be the god of sleep and dreams. Having read that, it came as no surprise to me as to where morphine got its name from. No one ever said the dreams were supposed to be pleasant...

Chapter 10
Prophecies Fulfilled

I must begin this chapter with a confession- I cheated on my bet with the doctor. There were times when the pain, as he very rightly foretold, was a little less than mind-numbing. But I was determined to hide my agony. I refused to let them know, lest they reinjected me with that hideous morphine. I chose the discipline of my senses over pain, and endured many waking hours of excruciating anguish so I could stay in control of what my eyes saw and my ears heard.

Eventually though, things started to look up, especially now that I was completely aware of my surroundings, and I alone governed my body. I decided that now would be a good a time as any to have as much long-overdue fun as possible. I was pretty much confined to the ward, so my only amusement would be to chew the matrons' brains, usually by frequently giving the 'call nurse' button a quality control test. Although my shenanigans were plentiful, one incident in particular remains fresh in my mind.

I called the nurse to my room.

"Hi, can I get a strawberry ice cream please?"

She stared at me as if I was asking her what planet she was from.

"Sir, it's three in the morning!" she remarked, looking at her watch, and then back at me.

"Oh!" I exclaimed, genuinely surprised, but it wasn't the first instance that I lost track of time. Strangely, it was the only thing I remained, for the most part, unaware of. "Well, I'd still love some," I said, grinning angelically.

Still in a state of disbelief, and clearly lacking the will to argue (smart woman), she replied, "I'll be right back."

And she was, with a small cup of half-melted, pink-colored gelato. After propping up my pillows, she proceeded to shut the door behind her, but not before giving me one last look of confusion and amusement.

It was not long, however, before she returned to my ward, this time looking completely annoyed, which, granted, she had a right to be. About a minute into my delectable dessert, the cup slipped from my hands and onto my not-in-the-least-bit-absorbent hospital gown. Feeling the cold liquid seep through the gown onto my legs, I wasn't sure which one of us was more pissed off. Sighing with exasperation, she left the ward without a single word, and returned seconds later with a new gown.

Just as she was about to help me change, one of the Filipino custodians entered my room.

"Sir, would you like some soap?" he asked politely (or at least, that's what I thought he'd asked me), having noticed the mess I'd made.

"That would be wonderful, thank you," I said. At least I'd be able to properly wash up. Nodding, he left the room.

Minutes passed, and even though I was in no hurry to get the soap as I was still being changed, I did start to wonder whether he'd gone to the laboratory to make a bar from scratch. Finally, ten minutes later, he returned, and the nurse and I exchanged confused looks- in his hands was a bowl, the contents of which were steaming.

What is that, a hot finger bowl?

He lay it down on my table, and I peered inside. Staring back at me was a clear, viscous liquid of a pale yellowish brown.

"Um…what is this, boss?" I enquired.

"You asked for soap, sir…this is fresh chicken soap."

The nurse and I exchanged humored looks, and then unable to control ourselves, we burst out laughing. The poor chap had no idea what we found so hilarious, and his look of confoundedness only tickled us more. Not knowing how to explain the joke to him without causing offence, I thanked him for the 'soap' and he left the ward, smiling, but still utterly confused. Bless his heart.

*

One morning, a female Pakistani doctor entered my room.

"Mr. Pervaiz, we need to get you to walk."

"Praise the Lord!" I exclaimed. I could have cried tears of joy at the thought of finally being mobile, even if to a small extent. "It's about bloody time!"

I recalled the words of Dr. Madhu from Qassimi that she had said to one of my friends- *'It will be at least six months before he can even put his foot down.'* I remember mentally replying to her: *In two months, doc, I will walk out of here on my own two feet.* I was elated; my prophecy was about to come true!

Ever so gingerly, I put my feet on the ground, my knees wobbling like jelly.

"The ground's spinning," I remarked, looking at her.

"Yes," she said, without a hint of anxiety in her tone. "Don't worry, I'd hardly expect you to 'get up and go' at this point. Just try to stand up holding the walker."

Nervously, I put both hands on either side of my cold, lifeless metal aid. Using all the strength I could muster, I heaved myself off the bed, letting all my weight fall onto the walker. My feet planted as firmly as possible on the ground, miraculously, I felt myself rise inches off the bed, until I made a ninety degree angle with the floor. In disbelief, I turned my head back and forth between my feet and the doctor, who beamed at me, vomiting endless words of praise and felicitations.

"*Mabrouk* (congratulations)! *Alhumdulillah* (glory be to God)! Well done, Pervaiz!" she exclaimed over and over again.

It certainly was a moment to celebrate. I could only stay standing for a few minutes though, as soon after, my legs buckled under me. But baby steps were to be expected at this stage of the recovery process. Slowly but surely, after three days of practising to stand, I was able to take my first steps. When I regained the energy to be a little more adventurous, I'd take my walker, or hold someone's hand, and trudge down the corridor to the nurses' station. There I'd stand flirting with them, in my sexy hospital gown that put my best *derrière* features on display for the viewing pleasure of hospital staff and patients alike. Finally, I'd be forced to return to my ward once the nurses expressed that they'd had enough of my corny lines, or when they noticed that other patients' conditions were worsening after being traumatized by the sight of my behind.

Weeks passed, and with time, I started to grow anxious. My mind dwelled upon a hallucination I had in Qassimi, one that involved my tiny green and blue feathered friend. It visited me in my room one day, and whispered in my ear, "Don't worry, you will be home in a maximum of two months." It had now been a little more than two months that I had been hospitalized and began to wonder whether that was a forecast I could believe, or whether I was holding on to false hopes.

Then came the morning of December 12th, my birthday. A team of doctors walked into my ward, and after exchanging pleasantries, they took their seats on the sofa cum bed. They then proceeded to chatter amongst themselves in hushed tones, until finally, one of them spoke up.

"Pervaiz, when would you like to go home?"

This was music to my ears. "What took you so long, Doc?" I replied. "I was due to be discharged the day before yesterday, so can someone just call me a freaking cab already?"

They all burst into laughter.

"OK, boss," said one, cheerfully. "As soon as the paperwork is ready, you are welcome to go home. It'll be a couple of hours, but I'm sure you and your behind can grace the nurses' station with your presence one last time."

It was my turn to laugh. I couldn't believe what I was hearing. After about eight weeks of the crappiest summer camp anyone could register for, I was finally able to go home. Shaking my hands, the doctors left my room, and soon after, Dr. Baqer visited me, completely jubilant.

"Pervaiz! Going home??!!" he exclaimed gleefully.

I saved my best handshake of the day for him, and thanked him profoundly for all he did for us.

He then sat down, and for about half and hour, ran me through all the dos and don'ts while back at home.

Finally, the hour of my departure from Rashid Hospital arrived, and I had the pleasure of being driven home by Amin and Pooja, and wheeled back into my apartment by my son. Awaiting me was a more than pleasant surprise- a birthday party that everyone had arranged for me. Mehru had organized the pomp and splendor of a traditional *Parsi* homecoming, and Tehmi had arranged a wide and scrumptious assortment of snacks. The warmest welcome of all, though, had to have come from Tinkerbell, my little princess. It was revealed that the initial plan was to have everyone come to the hospital, but due to a delay in the paperwork, the party had to be shifted to our place. No complaints though; a hospital is no place to celebrate a birthday, and I sincerely feel for anyone who has to commemorate such a joyous occasion in a hospital.

This would be a perfect conclusion to the book, and I so wish this could have been my happy ending, but alas, Satan had to have his way. A second deck of cards was about to be laid out across the table, and this diabolical game of chance was just getting started.

CHAPTER 11
BACK UNDER

On January 12th 2008, I woke up with a start, heaving, gasping for air, but it just didn't seem to enter my body. I tried swallowing my saliva, coughing, thinking something could have been stuck in my airways, but nothing seemed to work.

Oh, c'mon, not again! What the Hell is this? Why can't I breathe? Why can't I swallow? Am I choking?

Frantically pulling off the covers and scrambling out of bed, I tried taking a few steps forward. By the time I arrived at my bathroom, which was ten feet away from my bed, I felt ready to collapse, as if I was a runner who had just completed a 150km sprint from Dubai to Abu Dhabi.

"Maz! *MAZ!*"

She awoke instantly- she's never been too sound a sleeper.

"What happened? What's wrong?"

"Call Dr. Baqer...I can't breathe properly..." I huffed.

She wasted no time. After making a few frantic calls, we tracked down his location. He was at the Neuro-Spinal Hospital in Jumeirah, one of the more upmarket areas in Dubai. Maz hastily got dressed, and before I knew it, I was taken for the most uncomfortable drive I'd ever experienced. Something was obstructing my windpipe, and every breath I took required more and more effort on my part.

We finally arrived at Neuro-Spinal, and after locating Dr. Baqer, who was both shocked and dismayed to see me in urgent need of medical assistance, the tests and exams began all over again. Dr. Ahmed, the head of the clinic, kept me under his supervision in the observatory room while we awaited results. I remember being instructed to remain as still as possible, as the slightest movement would get me heaving again.

After hours of nervously anticipating test results, they concluded that I needed to be readmitted to the ICU.

Here we go again...

*

Days passed, seemingly at a slower pace than usual. I'd request the air conditioning to be on full blast in my room, but it still felt like a furnace at times, which made breathing all the more problematic. Finally, an electric pedestal fan was set up in my ward at maximum speed, perpetually facing me. Sandra, the head of the ICU, ran the nurses' station like a Major General on the battle front, bellowing orders, keeping all her soldiers on their toes.

I underwent one test after another, but they showed no signs of anything out of the ordinary. Day by day, doctors would ponder over me, huddling around me, trying to decipher what it was that was obstructing my air passage, and every test result would leave them baffled. Try as they might have, no one seemed to be able to pinpoint the problem, and the look of utter puzzlement on the doctors' faces didn't help in the slightest.

At long last, just when I was wondering whether I'd ever get a rational explanation as to why I was back in hospital, on the 23rd, Dr. Alaa Saleh's CT scan and radiology report revealed:

A segment of altered tracheal lumen being partially collapsed and flattened from side to side, with ill definition of its cartilaginous framework at its upper end, below the level of the thyroid gland; a localized thickening of the posterior and the right posterolateral aspect of the tracheal outline.

Dr. Baqer, who had received a copy of the report, translated it for me.

"In English," he said, "it means you have a small granulation growing on the inner walls of your trachea."

"OK. What do we do about it?" I asked.

"We'll have to place a stent in your trachea," came the reply.

"I'm sorry, a *what*?" Maz asked.

"A stent," repeated Dr. Baqer. "It's a foreign body that will basically hold the walls of the trachea up and apart, which should hopefully allow him to breathe normally."

"Fair enough," I chirped. I was just glad to finally be getting answers. "How soon will this be done?"

"I couldn't say. It depends on how quickly we can find where to send you," he said, frowning slightly.

"I don't quite follow," piped up Maz immediately, although her tone seemed to say, "I don't like where this is going."

"We don't have the medical or the technological expertise to deal with this kind of surgery, I'm afraid," he explained. "And by 'we', I mean the United Arab Emirates. The service is just not available here."

"So…what are we supposed to do?" Maz asked, dreading the response.

"We'll have to start researching where you can go, keeping in mind travel and visa costs and times, affordability and reputations of the hospitals under consideration."

With that, Maz buried her face in her hands. "This is just what we need," she said, despairingly.

*

Our network of friends and family went into hyper-drive as the search for a hospital with the necessary facilities began. Frantic phone calls were made across the world. Some pointed to India, which sounded good at first since we have friends and family there, but at the time, being a Pakistani national, it would have probably been easier to complete a PhD in nuclear physics than obtain an Indian visa. Others recommended Jordan, but we knew no one there, and needed the support of people we were acquainted with while in a foreign country. The U.K. seemed to be our most viable option. Tehmi started searching for hospitals with the most advanced facilities, and our friends Carole Spiers and Michael began researching doctors of repute.

Just when we were about ready to fill out the necessary paperwork to have me transported to the U.K., Dr. Baqer intervened.

"Wait, hold on a minute," he beamed, clutching a few sheets of paper, beaming.

"What's up, Doc?" I asked.

"You don't need to go. You can get the procedure done here!" he exclaimed, brandishing the papers in Maz's face.

"Where? Neuro-Spinal?" Maz asked excitedly.

"No, not *here* here, but in the Emirates. The Tawam Hospital in Al-Ain has just recently introduced the new technology needed for this procedure."

"Do you think they're credible?" she enquired, browsing through the papers.

"They're affiliated with John Hopkins in the States, so I'm sure they are."

"Who is this 'Dr. Jack Borders'?" Maz pondered out loud, still buried in the documents.

"Apparently one of the highest acclaimed otolaryngologists in his field," replied Dr. Baqer. "He used to be a resident doctor at John Hopkins, and he's currently practicing at Tawam. I suppose he'll be the one you'd need to speak to."

With that, Maz, Natasha, and Adil rushed to Al-Ain to meet with the legendary Dr. Jack Borders in person.

*

They encountered him in one of the hospital's many winding corridors, after he had just finished with a surgery. After being debriefed with my case, and reading the reports, he smiled.

"Bring him in," he said determinedly. We'll definitely be able to sort this out."

"Really?" said Maz, her eyes glistening with hope.

He nodded reassuringly. "All he needs is a stent to keep his airways from collapsing. If he's ready for it, the surgery can take place within a few days. He should be fine."

Elated, the three thanked him and rushed back to Dubai.

*

They managed to book the surgery for the day-after-next, and so by the following afternoon, I found myself in an ambulance, being transported to Tawam. They had me wait in the emergency waiting area while a room was being prepared, and by nightfall, I was wheeled into a double-occupancy private ward. The two beds were separated by a curtain, but no other patient was with me at the time, so Maz and I were alone.

It must have been around midnight or so, when an elderly matron entered my room with some pills.

"Son, you need to take these- they will stabilize you for tomorrow."

"You make me sound like a time-bomb about to explode," I remarked, chuckling, holding out my palm.

"They're to normalize your breathing and help you sleep, but I'm glad to see you still have a sense of humor," she replied, grinning.

"Wouldn't dare lose it. What time is the surgery again?"

"Eight a.m," she replied, after double-checking her clipboard.

"Excellent."

"You have a pleasant night now," she said, turning towards the door.

"You as well, and thank you for everything."

Just as she was about to shut the door behind her, Maz called after her.

"I'm sorry, but I suddenly remembered- where is Dr. Borders?"

"Gone for the day, Madam. Is there a problem?"

"No...not really," Maz began, apparently bemused, "but won't he need to see Pervaiz before the surgery?"

"He hasn't already?"

"No, Pervaiz has never met him..."

"Well, I suppose there was no explicit need to, then. He'll see him tomorrow in the operating room."

"OK," said a not-entirely-convinced Maz. "I find that a little odd, but, well, goodnight then…"

"Goodnight, Madam. All the very best for tomorrow, sir," she called out to me.

"Thank you," I replied, and she left.

Still looking a little perplexed, Maz turned towards me. I shared her confusion and concern.

"Bit odd, don't you think honey?"

"Shupposhe sho," I said yawning, "but you know what? Who the Hell cares? As long as he knows what he's doing…compared to the shit I've gone through already, this sounds like a walk in the park."

And with that final thought, I said whatever prayers I could in my mind before the drugs started to take effect and my eyes began to droop. The last thing I remember before completely shutting down was my cheek being tenderly kissed, and Maz sweetly whispering 'I love you' in my ear. I had just enough strength left to curve my lips into a smile before I thought no more.

*

Come 7:00a.m, with great difficulty, I shaved, showered and wore a new gown. Whilst dressing, I could constantly hear my wife tsk-tsk away.

"Pervaiz," Maz said, concerned, "you're going for surgery, not to the ball. Can you please not exhaust yourself unnecessarily?"

"Honey, I can't risk the doctor fainting while my throat's opened up."

"Why would he faint?" she asked, surprised.

Grinning, I replied, "That's why I showered."

We both laughed. At about 7:30, my nurse-drawn stretcher-carriage arrived at the door, and I was wheeled into the operating arena.

The atmosphere was less serious than I had anticipated. Doctors and nurses were joking with each other, and everyone seemed rather jovial, and very friendly. I guess that's how they keep the patient's nerves under control. They told me to get into the most comfortable position I could, and helped me each and every step, adjusting my hands, legs, head…whatever I'd ask. One of the nurses enquired as to whether I was nervous. I chuckled to myself, recalling everything I'd been through so far. After those harrowing hallucinations back in Qassimi at the very least, did I really need to be?

A few seconds later, a tall, big-built man entered the room. He approached my side, and extended his hand. I must say, it was a very firm handshake.

"I'm Jack Borders, my friend. Give me about forty minutes- I'll have you breathing normally."

His confidence was remarkable, which made it all the easier to relax.

A soft voice whispered in my ears, "Shhh… now look at the clock in front of you, we're about to put you to sleep."

I giggled, instantly imagining a hypnotist swinging a pocket watch before his subject's eyes. I was tempted to try and fight off the effects of the anesthesia, just to mess with the medical team. I closed my eyes, pretending to cooperate with the surgeons, but just then, I felt a gentle slap of a hand against my cheek.

"Hey, Pervaiz! C'mon, wake up! It's time to take you back to your room."

"What?" I said groggily, opening my surprisingly heavy eyelids. "Are you insane? I just got here! Where is Dr. Borders?"

The assistant laughed. "Last I heard he was having a cup of coffee in the staff canteen."

"Aha...and pray tell, what about my stent?" I enquired, blatantly exaggerating my politeness. The whole conversation sounded absolutely absurd.

Am I hallucinating again?

"The surgery was completed about an hour ago, boss. You've been asleep all this time."

I had a really good laugh. So much for trying to fight the anesthesia...Still drowsy, I was wheeled back to my room. I passed Adil and Natasha in the corridor, giving them both a high-five. Maz was waiting for me in the ward, ready to fling her arms around me.

"Guys, can you send for a McDonald's meal for me please?" I requested, embracing my wife.

They chuckled, thinking I was probably still not out of it, but I do remember that I felt hungry enough to eat a horse. Perhaps this was an effect of the anesthesia…? But one thing's for certain- when I woke up after sleeping for another two hours or so, I felt like a million dollars. The feeling you get after waking up from being knocked out by the drug is unmatchable.

Recovery time was just a few days, but they were painful. So painful in fact that I was forced to take another dose of that hideous narcotic, morphine. Thankfully, the dose was not too large, so the hallucinations were not as bizarre or dreadful as what I had already experienced back at Qassimi, save for one.

It involved my angel, Tinkerbell. She had died due to a heat stroke while serving as our new family gardener. Weird, I know. Anyway, I would just not heed my family's assurances that she was alive and well. As a result, they brought her all the way to Al Ain so I could see her for myself and put my mind at ease. Of course, she wouldn't be allowed inside the hospital, but I was allowed to meet her at the entrance on the lawn. Her perkiness and frolicking spirit were endearing, and it was an ardent joy to see her. The rest of the recovery period remained more or less uneventful.

After thanking the hospital staff for all their hard work and great service, I was on my way back home, fit as a fiddle. No more heaving or huffing, feeling short of breath or as if I was about to faint- it was such a relief to be able to breathe normally again. Adil had arranged for his office car and driver to take us home. On the way, I telephoned my bosses at work, and they were relieved to know that all was well again.

Being home again was indeed a cause for celebration. I was required to go for periodic check-ups back to Tawam, and would be seen by either Dr. Borders or Dr. Anjum Naveed, one of the other doctors assigned to my case. Things looked nice and rosy for a while, and soon enough, we started to feel all would be well from here on. If only that was the case…as our luck would have it, Satan was not ready to give up. The card table was being reset, and he was preparing to trump me with his Ace.

CHAPTER 12
ORAL TRADITIONS

While I was still feeling up to the mark, I decided now would be a good time to get some dental work done. After all, there was quite a substantial amount of damage: two broken front teeth and extensive injury to my molars and jaws on either side. I began regular consultations with our family dentist, Dr. Nozar Bamboat, to see just how much of the problem could be fixed.

"Pervaiz, just how do you want me to get any work done if you can't keep your head still for me?" Dr. Bamboat chuckled one day while trying to examine my jaws.

"I'm sorry Doc," I said, sincerely, snatching the paper towel away from my neck and readjusting myself in the dentist chair, "but that's just it: I can't keep my head back in this position for long. It begins to hurt my throat. It's probably the stent or something."

Dr. Bamboat thought for a minute, then shrugged his shoulders in despair.

"I honestly don't know what else to tell you, Pervaiz. We'll just have to wait for your throat to completely heal before you come back for any more treatment. There's really no point to this otherwise."

"I don't know how long that will take. It could be months before my throat's completely normal again," I said in dismay.

"You have a better idea, boss?"

"Let's just see how much we can get done right now. I'll stay as still as I can."

"Alright...your call," replied Dr. Bamboat, frowning slightly.

But a few minutes into the checkup, I had to stop. The pain in my throat was starting to become unbearable while my head remained in that awkward position.

"No, Pervaiz, enough," he said adamantly, removing his gloves and disposing of them.

"We'll have to wait this out. I can't ask you to endure this kind of discomfort."

"I've been through worse, believe me Doc," I replied, stubbornly.

"Nevertheless, let's be patient. Why don't you contact your doctor and tell him this is happening? If it's normal, fine, but if something's wrong, don't you think he should know about it?"

Though I hated myself for giving in, I did find some wisdom in his words, and proceeded to get up from the chair.

"Alright, Doc, I know when I'm defeated."

"Smart fellow. I just hope we can get it done sooner rather than later."

"Are you looking busier down the line, or leaving town for a while…?"

"No, but with the condition your jaws are in, prolonging treatment can lead to complications later on. I'd hate to be in your shoes should that happen."

"Oh, for sure. No, we'll get this done as soon as possible," I said, extending my hand for his.

"Right, Pervaiz, you keep well, and we'll try this again when you're feeling more up to it. And do keep me informed about what your doctor said."

"Sure thing, Doc. Thanks so much for everything."

And with that, I left the clinic. Sensible as it might have been to revisit Dr. Borders and tell him about this tingling in my throat, I decided to shrug it off as simply a part of the healing process. Like many men, I make it a habit to wait until the time a doctor really needs to intervene before involving one.

And then, April came, along with the very same problem that started it all.

Oh, dear God, not again! I BEG you!

Once more, I felt like a cross-country runner who just completed a run from Dubai to Abu Dhabi non-stop. Once more, someone may as well have had their hand gripping my neck; I couldn't breathe properly.

"Maz..."

"Sweetheart, why are you panting like that?" she asked anxiously.

"Don't know...call Dr. Borders..." I heaved.

Within minutes, we were on our way back to Tawam. The memories of my first ride to Al Ain came flooding back as I relived the discomfort.

Back at the hospital, after an examination, Dr. Borders realized that the pain was a result of tissue scarring around the walls of my trachea.

"It's easy enough to deal with though," he assured us. "We'll have to use laser treatment to target the scars, but that should heal them."

It really was that simple. Following a session of laser therapy was a recovery period of just about three days, after which I was back home, and the uneasiness in my throat did seem to subside. It also helped normalize my breathing. But weeks later, the problem arose again, and I found myself back at Tawam for another session of laser treatment under Dr. Borders' supervision. And just when we thought we wouldn't have to go back for a third round, the pain recommenced. Over the period of roughly eight to ten months, I underwent three sessions of laser treatment for trachea tissue scarring. But that was the least of my troubles. One day during these many months, Ardavan backed away from me, a look of utter disgust on his face.

"Dear God, Dad, *what is that smell*?"

"It wasn't me, I swear!" I exclaimed, defending myself.

"Dad, there's some God-awful stench coming from you!"

I stood there, both bemused and unamused, my eyebrows coming together.

"What are you on about? I showered today!" I protested, smelling my armpits.

But Ardavan persisted.

"No, Dad, from your *mouth*!"

I was really confused now.

"My *mouth*?"

I breathed out from my mouth into my hand and inhaled. Nothing.

"Sweetheart," I called out to Maz, "can you check if there's there some foul smell coming from my mouth?"

My wife looked at me as if I was speaking Greek.

"Do I look stupid? Wait, don't answer that."

"Honey, I'm serious," I protested, growing more and more frustrated.

"So am I!" Maz replied. "Don't ask me to smell your mouth! If someone says there's a foul odor coming from your mouth, you brush your teeth, silly, don't ask others to verify!"

My daughter, who was in the room with us, could no longer contain herself. She burst out into a seemingly unending fit of laughter.

"Fine! I'll eat a bloody breath mint!"

"Please brush your teeth!" cried Ardavan, still clutching his nose, as if it were about to fall off.

"Stop being such a drama king!" I snapped.

"I MEAN IT!" he yelled.

He really did. Not having the energy to argue, I proceeded to the bathroom and brushed. When I thought I'd done a good enough job, I returned to Ardavan and shoved my mouth in his face.

"Better?" I demanded.

"Much!" he exclaimed, after taking the smallest whiff he could, and then continuing his work on his laptop.

I went back to my room, shrugging the entire incident off as the result of poor oral hygiene, that is, until Maz walked by me in the corridor a few hours later.

"Dear God!" she exclaimed.

"What happened?" I asked.

"What on *Earth* is that smell?"

"I swear, Maz, if you tell me there's some rotten smell coming from my mouth-"

"There *is*! How can you not smell it?" she asked, completely bewildered.

And without being told to, I headed back to the bathroom and brushed my teeth for the third time that day (and it wasn't even lunch time).

What is this smell that everyone's raving about, and why the fuck can't I smell it?

The rest of the day passed by without another complaint regarding an alien odor, thank God. But my peace of mind was short-lived; the next day, the madness resumed, with everyone around me shielding their noses and running for the hills. There was just one difference- this time, I could smell it too.

"Glory be to God!" I cried.

"What did I tell you?" Maz said nasally, clutching her nostrils. "Maybe you should see Dr. Bamboat about this. Perhaps it has to do with your gums or something."

"Yeah, maybe…" I thought out loud.

I quickly booked the next available appointment with him, and a few days later, was back in his room, in that usually fun, but now annoying chair. After discussing the issue with him, Dr. Bamboat, even while wearing his face mask, placed his nose close to my mouth, and nearly toppled over.

"Bloody Hell! What is that stench?"

"That's what I was hoping you'd be able to tell me, Doc," I replied gloomily.

Heaving away from me, he mumbled something about investing in fragranced face masks, and then turned towards me.

"I can check, but I doubt I'll find anything that could explain this. I've seen your teeth and gums before, there was nothing that have caused your mouth to stink up like that."

Taking a deep breath and then locking the air in his lungs, he rolled his chair towards me, and began probing at my teeth, tongue and gums with his apparatus. After a few minutes of a thorough inspection, interrupted only by his gasping for a new intake of air, he shook his head and shrugged.

"Sorry, Pervaiz, but I can't understand where this smell is coming from," he said hopelessly.

"But what do I do? The family can't stand to be near me sometimes!"

"Mouthwash? A new toothpaste, perhaps? They should provide some temporary relief, but I doubt this is a dental issue to begin with."

If it's not a dental issue, then what the fuck is it? Why can't anyone figure out the problem?

I trudged along home. I took Dr. Bamboat's advice and started using a mouthwash, but as he said, it proved to be only a temporary solution. Within a few hours of gargling with it, the stink would resurface. With no one able to detect the source of this bizarre, horrific odor, there was nothing to do but wait to see what would happen.

Hopefully, whatever it was, time would take care of it.

*

It was now around May 2009, and not too surprisingly, the day came when I found I'd need yet another session of laser therapy with Dr. Borders, as my throat started acting up again. What did come as a bit of a shock, though, was what we discovered when we called the hospital to make an appointment.

"I'm sorry, Pervaiz, but Dr. Borders is no longer with us," said Dr. Naveed.

"Um…when you say 'no longer with us', what do you mean?" I asked, not too sure of what to expect.

"I mean he's left the hospital, and the U.A.E. He's back in the States. His replacement will be taking over your case."

"And who would that be?"

"Dr. Francis Stafford. Don't worry, you'll be in good hands."

I had no doubt of it. I had never had a bad experience with any of the doctors who tended to me so far, so why should Dr. Stafford have been any different?

*

"Before we do anything, I'd like to examine you for myself, just so I get a clear picture of what I'm working with," Dr. Stafford told us.

"Whatever you say, Doc," I replied.

I followed him to the examination room, leaving Maz and Ardavan to chat in the ward.

He scrutinized my throat for over an hour. I still remember the annoying discomfort of a laryngoscopy. He'd spend minutes staring at his miniature TV screen, completely enraptured, and then hastily jot down his observations with furious concentration, probably in that signature penmanship only doctors can decipher. The examination passed in almost pin-drop silence. Finally, he removed the tube from my nostrils, turned off the TV screen, grabbed a pile of papers off his desk, and beckoned me out of the room, and we proceeded back to the ward.

"I can see the damage done, but I'm afraid I cannot know just how bad it is unless I open you up," he told us.

"And by 'open you up', you mean surgery, right?" I asked needlessly. He nodded.

"I don't understand," said Maz, shaking her head. "All he needed was the routine laser treatment for the scarring tissues…"

Looking momentarily bemused, Dr. Stafford responded, "Oh no, we're way past that. Did you ever detect a foul smell coming from his mouth?"

"*YES!*" Ardavan exclaimed, almost excitedly. "We've been trying to figure out what it is, but for the life of us, we don't know."

"He's been going to the dentist for that. We thought it might have something to do with rotting gums," explained Maz. "Why, do you know what it is?" she asked, her eyes glistening with hope.

"Indeed I do," replied Dr. Stafford, gravely. He turned to me. "It's not your rotting gums- it's your rotting trachea."

The room was silent as a tomb for a moment. He took that as his cue to keep explaining the situation.

"Your trachea has been trying to heal, but it's started doing so around the stent's wire," he continued. "In the sense, the wire has begun poking through the walls of the trachea. That has led to a fungus, which has led to rotting. But as I said, I need to put you on the surgery table. There's no way for me to be sure how bad the situation is just by doing a laryngoscopy. It shouldn't take too long; I'd probably be done in about forty or forty-five minutes."

Maz and I exchanged nervous looks. "When on Earth did this fungus start to develop?" she thought out loud.

As much as I didn't like the sound of being put back on the operating table, what option did I have? We got through all the formalities, and arranged for me to go back under the surgeon's knife.

*

I opened my eyes, slowly and groggily as the anesthesia started to wear off. I was back in the ward, and something or someone was caressing my forehead. It was Maz.

"It's OK, sweetheart, you'll be OK soon," she said, tenderly.

Frowning slightly, my eyes darted to the wall clock. It had been much, much longer than forty-five minutes since I was wheeled in for surgery. Try four and a half *hours*.

"Maz, what happened? Why did it-"

What the bloody fuck? Where'd my voice go? Why am I wheezing?

"Honey, it'll probably hurt to talk right now, so don't strain yourself."

She was right; there was a slight pain in my throat, but what of it?

What happened to my voice? And what is this shit in my neck?

My hand scurried to my throat, frantically feeling its way along something long and plastic jutting out of it.

"No, sweetie, don't touch it! LEAVE IT ALONE!"

Maz had to grasp my hand in hers and wrench it away from my throat. Pushing her hands aside, I scrambled out of bed, ignoring how tired my body still felt, and rushed to the bathroom. I hastily switched on the light and turned towards the mirror. Sticking two, maybe three inches out of my neck was a small, white tube, taped in place by bandages. I had no idea what this was, or why it was there, but I was sure I wasn't going to like the reasoning behind it. And then, only after staring at myself for a few seconds did I realize that no air was going into my body through my nose. My nostrils just weren't inhaling.

Is this tube supposed to be my new air passage? How long will this be in here?

I could have screamed, or at least, I wanted to, but for starters, it would probably have hurt like Hell, and second, who would have been able to hear me?

I returned to Maz, pointing to the tube in disbelief.

"I know, sweetheart, I know," she said comfortingly.

"Where's Dr. Stafford?" I wheezed.

"He'll be here tomorrow to properly explain everything, honey. For now, please try to relax, and whatever happens, don't unnecessarily try to talk. You'll exhaust yourself, and your throat's gone through enough for one day."

There was no point in arguing. Talking hurt, Maz didn't know the entire story, and the doctor would be able to inform us of what was going on only the next day. Resorting to hand gestures, pointing, writing, miming, text messaging and whatever other forms of non-verbal communication I could imagine, I got through the day, until 9:00 a.m the following morning.

*

Dr. Stafford pulled up a chair, placed it next to my bed, and took a seat beside me.

"Pervaiz, your internal condition was far worse than what the laryngoscopy could show, or what I had imagined. The wire mesh of the stent had merged so brilliantly with the walls of your trachea that I was unable to remove it without removing a part of the trachea itself. Tracheostomy was my only option. For the time being, you'll need that tube to help you breathe."

We were dumbstruck. Silence filled the room, and he continued.

"The fungal infection had started to spread, and a fatal bacteria formed. I'm very glad we got this done now; had you waited a couple of days, you probably would not have made it out alive."

The only audible sound was Ardavan's heavy breathing. The news undoubtedly shook him up a little.

I wrote on a sheet of paper, 'How long will I need this tube? When will I be able to talk again?'

Dr. Stafford sighed. "I wish I could tell you, Pervaiz, but I really don't know. It could be a month, maybe two…or, you might have to live with this."

I opened my mouth in disbelief, before penning down '4eva?' and showing it to him. He nodded dismally.

"I'm sorry, I wish I had better news," he said, sympathetically, getting up to leave. "Try to get some rest, and stick to the pad and paper for now. Don't unnecessarily exert your throat if you want it to heal quickly. Let's hope for the best."

With that, he turned towards the door, and was almost out of the ward when I banged on the bed railing to grab his attention. He spun around, and his eyes fell upon the 'Thank u for saving my life' that I wrote on the paper. He smiled, shaking his head.

"It wasn't me. You have God to thank for the fact that you're still alive, but as far as I'm concerned, I lost you about thirty minutes into the surgery."

He left the ward, silence in his wake, leaving the three of us to our thoughts.

CHAPTER 13

FLAVORLESS ROCKY ROAD

Recovery…dear Lord, recovery was a roller coaster ride. I was, without question, grateful to be alive. Who knows what could have happened had the fungus spread any more than it did? I was blessed to be surrounded by such a knowledgeable, compassionate and humble medical team. And of course, having my family by my side throughout made the ordeal ten times more bearable.

My family would make the two-and-a-half-hour trip from Dubai to Al Ain every day, stay with me for a few hours, and then return home. It was especially lovely to see my mother-in-law, who visited me as often as thrice a week at times. Mehru would enter my room, hug me as tightly as she could without breaking her feeble bones, and then take a seat next to me, clutching her prayer book for at least an hour. At times, one of Maz, Nasha or Ardavan would spend the night in the ward with me. No doubt my family went to great lengths to smoothen the recovery process for me, but still, for a variety of reasons, it was easier going through the problem than putting up with the solution.

I remember the look of pure terror on everyone's face when we experienced it for the first time. I was in the middle of penning something down for my family to read, when all of a sudden, I started coughing. Violently. At first, we thought nothing of it, and assumed it would simply pass. After establishing the contrary, however, just as my fingers started heading towards the 'call nurse' button, something shot out of the tracheostomy tube like a bullet and attached itself on the wall across me. With that, the coughing began to subside.

Nasha screamed, Maz clapped her hands over her mouth, and Ardavan looked like he'd seen a ghost. That thing on the wall resembled a piece of raw chicken liver. Ardavan started to approach it.

"Be careful, don't get too near it!" Maz shrieked.

"For Heaven's sake, Mom, it's not gonna bite!" he snapped. He proceeded towards it, and we watched in disgust as the article started sliding down the wall. His nose was almost touching it when he said, "It's some red, white and yellow shit."

"Yes, thank you, can you come back now please?" implored Maz, not caring a bit for what colors decked the gunk.

"Whatever this is, it's got blood in it," said Ardavan, completing his analysis, and proceeding towards the door.

"Where are you going?" I asked.

"Nurses' station, where else?"

Minutes later, he returned with a nurse who was carrying a contraption that resembled a miniature vacuum cleaner, and a bottle of clear liquid.

"OK, the tube's getting clogged," she announced.

"With what?" Nasha asked.

"Food particles, saliva…all you need to do is clean it on a regular basis with this suction device," she instructed, holding the mini-vacuum up for all to see. "Turn it on, insert this suction pipe into the tube and wait for all the grit and grime to come out. Don't push the pipe in too deep or he might choke. Then clean the suction pipe by vacuuming some saline through it," she explained, pointing to the bottle. She then turned to me.

"Sorry, but you're going to have to go on a liquid and baby food diet. They'll be easier on your throat."

"For how long?" I asked, dreading the response.

"I wouldn't start a countdown just yet. Don't worry, we have all the ice-cream and jelly you can eat. And as long as it's easy to swallow, your family can bring you home-cooked stuff too."

I flopped my head back into my pillow.

Un-bloody-believable.

She was just about to head out the door when she took a sharp turn back towards us.

"Oh, and no greasy or fatty foods either. I also wouldn't recommend anything very spicy."

"You know what, why don't I just go vegan?" I retorted.

She thought for a moment, and shrugging her shoulders said, "That's actually not a bad idea."

I could have thrown something at her. Sensing my blood starting to boil, she smiled at me, chuckling to herself, and left the room. I instantly turned to my wife with my signature unhappy puppy-dog face. With my eyes widened, full of hope, and my lips contorted into a grossly exaggerated frown, I squeaked, "McDonald's burger...?"

Maz grinned from ear to ear. Laughing, she leaned forward, kissed my cheek, and said, "As many as you want sweetheart, as soon as you're out of this."

For some reason, I liked the first part of the sentence more than the second.

A routine diet of bland mashed potatoes, ice-cream and jelly became the least of my concerns. Walking was once again a nightmarish task. I don't know whether I should attribute it to the medication, or the presence of the tube jutting out of my neck, but I felt so completely out of balance. With every step I'd take, I felt as if I was seconds from falling forward, as if gravity grabbed me by the ears and pulled me down. Dizzy as it made me, I was determined to not become bedridden, and made sure that I walked a few steps every day. Eventually, I found myself patrolling through the corridors of the hospital, and at times, even exiting the building and sitting on one of the lawn benches, watching the sun set.

Arguably the most frustrating problem I had to endure was the disappearance of my voice, and the fact that I had to rely on writing or texting to make myself understood. Not being able to hold a real conversation with anyone made me feel so utterly disconnected from the rest of the world. Nasha was the only one who could lip-read, whereas my wife, son, and most of the medical staff definitely needed to spend some time honing the skill.

Days passed by, excruciatingly slowly. There were times where I'd literally stare at the clock, watching the red seconds hand tick by, eagerly anticipating the movement of the minute-hand. Nasha brought me a laptop and the entire '24' series to help pass time. I remember completing the first season over the span of twenty-four hours, to make the experience all the more realistic. Eventually, sleep would take me over, and I'd take a break, before continuing on to season two the next day. Occasionally, I'd try my hand at crosswords, word-searches and other such mentally stimulating puzzles to keep my mind from rotting away.

Eventually, I started to have regular sessions with Dr. Toni Arndell, a senior speech pathologist, who would come to my room on an almost daily basis, and teach me to effectively communicate without putting too much strain on my throat. She was kind, patient, understanding and compassionate. Each morning, she'd assure me that the whole scenario was temporary, and that the tube would soon be out, giving me back my regular voice.

Thankfully, after a painful four-week span, I was allowed to return home when the staff realized that my children were able to clean the tracheostomy tube with the suction device on their own. There was no real need for me to linger around in the hospital; I could take my medication orally, and breathe, eat and walk unaided, and as long as I continued this way, there was little point in me sitting idle in the hospital, wondering whether it was genuine fatigue or boredom that was wearing me out.

*

My first week at home was extremely uncomfortable, but I eventually grew accustomed to it. Being surrounded by familiar sights, smells and sounds definitely proved to be a catalyst in the recovery process. My patience was definitely tested when I could smell my wife's delectable cooking, especially when I watched everyone else enjoy it while I was stuck with what was essentially bland mush. There were times when I'd give into temptation, and not care how painful it was to eat real food, or the fact that the tube might get clogged. I'd nibble at bread, rice, meat...basically, anything and everything that the nurse would have prohibited. Sorry to say it was my family who paid the price for it, especially Ardavan, who took on the messy, smelly task of performing the tube-cleaning ritual most often, donning the surgical gloves, mask and hair cover. There was an instance or two when the tube got so clogged that the suction couldn't handle removing all the blockage, and I ended up coughing it up onto my son.

Despite not being completely healed, I decided to bring back as much routine to my life as I could, and resumed my work at the bank. The pain in my throat did hinder my ability to talk for very long though, which, being in customer service and client care, formed pretty much the bulk of my work. So I'd sit in the corner getting as much as I could accomplished without having to talk too much, while a colleague took over some of my clients for me. I was content with the normalcy returning, and I'm sure that aided the recovery process. Slowly but surely, my life started to see a hint of color again.

After roughly a month, the day arrived when we needed to see how well, if at all, the healing process was coming along. I found myself back in Tawam eagerly awaiting Dr. Stafford's verdict.

"Has it healed? Can I get rid of this God-forsaken contraption?"

"We shall see, Pervaiz, we shall see," said Dr. Stafford.

So back on his table I went so he could properly assess the situation. To my dismay, however, when I awoke, the tube was still in place. Dr. Stafford, however, beamed at me.

"It's healing very well. Just give it a little more time. I need you to come back to the hospital for a while now, just so I can monitor it more closely. And for goodness' sake, remain silent as much as you can. Let's not unnecessarily tax the trachea, especially when it's starting to show promise."

Later on, when I communicated to Dr. Arndell what Dr. Stafford had told me, she was thrilled. At times, she seemed more excited than I was.

"I'm sure this will all work out, Pervaiz. We just need to be a little more patient."

"Hopefully I'll have my voice back soon," I whispered.

Dr. Arndell laughed. "What do you mean 'hopefully'? I need to hear you narrate your entire story from start to finish, so it had bloody-well better come back!"

Chapter 14

His Last Ace

A few days later, one of the nurses entered my ward.

"Sir, Dr. Stafford would like a word with you."

I beckoned for her to show him in, but she shook her head.

"No, sir, he's on the phone," she clarified.

Bemused, I pulled off my sheets, clambered out of bed and followed the nurse back to the nurses' station.

"Hello?" I whispered. I couldn't talk normally just yet, but I had progressed to being able to whisper, which made my family tingle with excitement.

"Pervaiz, please tell one of the nurses to plug the tube for you. We have to see if you can breathe through your nose now. I'll call back in a few hours."

Click.

If there was an award for 'shortest phone conversation'…and what does he mean 'plug the tube'?

I informed the nurse of what Dr. Stafford said to me. She nodded and we both proceeded back to my ward.

"Just what exactly are you going to do?" I asked, sitting down on the bed.

"Exactly what Dr. Stafford said, sir: plug the tube," she said, showing me a small object that looked like a bottle cap. "If we're to see if you can breathe through your nose or not, we need to make sure air cannot travel through the tracheostomy tube."

That made sense. She screwed the cap over the opening of the tune, and I looked at her in anticipation.

"You'll have to breathe, sir," she said, trying to stifle a laugh.

"Oh, right!" I said foolishly.

I inhaled, and instantly felt something cool rush into my nostrils. I gasped, turning my head towards the nurse, hardly daring to believe it. I inhaled deeply again, as if taking in some heavenly scent. My lips started curving into the widest grin I'd smiled in a long time.

"Once more, just to be sure…" said the nurse, excitedly.

I obliged, and we were elated with the results. Leaving the tube covered, she left me in the ward, allowing me to bask in my delight. Later that evening, I was back at the nursing station on the phone with Dr. Stafford.

"Alright doc, we plugged the tube, and I can breathe normally. *Now* can you get rid of this thing?"

"Sorry, Pervaiz, I can't do that right now," came a gloomy response.

"What? Why not?"

"Because you'll have to do it yourself," he said, chuckling.

I could not believe what I was hearing. "Are you serious?"

"Absolutely! Just sit on a chair, put a plastic sheet over your lap, then hold the tube in one hand and pull. There'll be a lot of blood and gore; just ignore it, and tell the nurse to bandage you up."

At this point, I was convinced one of us was losing our brain cells at an alarmingly exponential rate, and began laughing hysterically.

"C'mon, Doc, really. When can you remove it?"

"Pervaiz, I've never been more serious," he insisted. "Really, just do what I told you."

"Whatever you say, Doc," I said skeptically, and hung up.

He couldn't have been serious, it's just not possible.

"He wants me to pull it out," I told the nurse who connected me to Dr. Stafford.

She shrugged her shoulders. "So what are you waiting for? Pull it out then!"

Has everyone in this hospital gone completely insane?

With nothing else for it, I returned to my room, fished out the plastic bag from the empty bin next to my bed, and draped it over my lap like a serviette. My eyes snapped shut as I took a deep breath, and my fingers clenched the tube.

3...2...1

In one swift movement, everything Dr. Stafford mentioned came hurdling out of my neck like a volcanic eruption. The plastic was strewn with blood, grime and tubes, but I didn't care. It was difficult for me to take in what had just happened- what had taken the doctors four and a half hours to achieve, I undid in less than four seconds! Absolutely elated and in minimal pain, I wrapped up the mess, tossed it into the bin, then ran back to the nurses' station, where the nurse was already holding a bandage for my wound.

"Did it work? Is my voice back? Can you hear me???" I demanded.

But I didn't need to hear a reply. *My voice! It's back! I CAN HEAR MYSELF!*

"Yes to all three!" she exclaimed beaming brighter than the sun.

It was difficult to suppress my tears. The joy I felt is far from describable; I could barely keep my balance, and was trembling with excitement. I asked the nurse to get Dr. Stafford back on the phone.

"I feel better than brand new, Doc. I don't know how to thank you," I said, sniffling slightly.

"Don't thank me, Pervaiz, really. I hardly did anything. It's great to hear your voice again!"

My next call was to Maz.

"Hi sweetheart," I said.

She squealed in delight, so loudly I'm sure the nursing station could hear her. I couldn't wait to see her and my family again, and finally be discharged from the hospital. I proceeded back to my ward and began calling half the world from my cellphone. Family, friends, colleagues… everyone I could possibly think of so I could share the good news.

I fell to my knees, hardly knowing what to say to Him. "Thank you," I whispered. Shortly after, Dr. Arndell visited me in the ward, grinning from ear to ear. She had obviously heard the news already.

"Alright, Pervaiz," she said after hugging me. "I have about twenty minutes before I have to be back at my desk." She pulled up a chair and sat down next to my bed. "As much as you can, from the top."

I knew exactly what she meant. "Fasten your seatbelt, Doc!" I chirped, grinning.

I wasn't able to finish the story in its entirety in those brief twenty minutes, but while I spoke, she remained silent as a mouse, completely mesmerized by my words. I did, however, reveal to her that I had started forming plans to document my experiences in the form of a novel.

"Any idea what you're going to call it?" she asked inquisitively.

I thought for a moment, and then said, "Trauma Redefined."

"I look forward to reading it," she said, beaming. With that, she got up, hugged me one last time, wished me well, and left the room.

After all the paperwork was arranged, signed and stamped, I bid the nurses and doctors goodbye, thanking them for all their efforts in keeping me alive and well, and left Tawam Hospital, hoping to never have to return, as a patient anyway.

There was one last thing to get done now that the tube was out and I could breathe normally: my dental work. I returned to Dr. Bamboat's clinic, and over the period of about five to six weeks, after a few implants and repairs done to both jaws, my teeth were back to normal. How I savored every morsel of my family's cooking from then on! Maz also made good on her promise, and I found myself eating one McDonald's burger after the other. I didn't want to see mashed potatoes and other such food for a while.

Even now, roughly eight years after all these events took place, I still wonder how I got through it. Chainsaws, birds, doppelgangers, tubes, machines, drugs, surgeries, angels, demons... it's impossible that I lived through all this and more by chance. Someone somewhere had to be guiding me, step by step through this entire saga. This game was rigged from the start. What chance could poor Satan possibly have hoped for when playing against God? I'll say one thing for him, though: he knows when he's defeated. He knows when to bow out gracefully, and he did, the minute I yanked that tube from my throat, when God trumped his last Ace.

MAH-ZARIN'S
NOTE OF THANKS

There are numerous people I would like to thank for all the support they showed us during this trying time: the Sharjah Police, for their efforts in my husband's case; the medical staff of the Qassimi Hospital, for their professionalism, compassion and sympathy for our predicament; my brother-in-law Adil and his wife Natasha (who found a way to be with us even though her own mother was on her deathbed in Pakistan), the Management of Habib Bank AG Zurich for looking after every need of their employee and his family, the Management of Emirates Airline, who was instrumental in securing him a place in Rashid Hospital; my ex-boss Tony Tayeh's unflinching support, and of course, most importantly, Dr. Baqer Ali, whose efforts ensured Pervaiz's acceptance into Rashid Hospital's ICU and treatment due to which Pervaiz got on his road to recovery. My gratitude to the staff of the Neuro Spinal Hospital Dubai, and finally, the Tawam Hospital in Al Ain, in order of hospitals that Pervaiz was admitted for his treatment of sorts. Dr Hina Mirza, Dr Nozer Bamboat, Dr Jack Borders, Dr Francis Stafford and Dr Naveed Malik- I am indebted to you all.

To my darling Mom Mehru – my Rock and Inspiration who I miss every single day, my beloved children Nasha and Ardavan who were always there for me, and my precious little Tinkerbell with her unconditional love, I thank you all immensely.

My humble gratitude to my Pervaiz's dear parents, to his dear aunt Roshan, my beloved cousins Tehmi and Sam, and our dearest friends Pouruchisty Sidhwa, Adil Irani, Samad Khan and Behram Mana who travelled to Dubai just to be with us.

There was hardly a time when our telephones would remain silent – such was the huge outpour of concern from those known to us, as well as from strangers who are now part of what I call our 'extended family'- Goolcher Navdar and our priest Darayus Dastur form a part of this list.

My deepest and most profound gratitude to the One whose door I knocked a million times over, sometimes gently and sometimes with a hundred blows, my Maker. No matter how hopeless the situation seemed, I felt, rather *saw* His divine presence every rocky step of the way; it manifested itself in all the love and support we were shown by people from all walks of life. He made me realize that I could put all my trust in Him and that He had been watching over Pervaiz from the very beginning. Every time Pervaiz's vitals went erratic, every time he came close to losing his life, I begged Him, pleaded with Him to keep my husband safe in His care, and He didn't turn me down. Such is the power of prayer and Divine intervention.

It is impossible for me to take the names of everyone, for it would be an exhaustive list, but thank you all from the bottom of my heart for your prayers and for your help, be it by way of arranging transportation, bringing cooked meals or just being there for us. God bless you all.

Mah-Zarin Pervaiz Taraporewala

EDITOR'S NOTE

The undertaking of this project has been nothing short of an emotional roller coaster ride. My father would draft up his thoughts, which I would then turn into prose. Upon reading what he'd provide me with, I found myself being humored, awed, shocked and at times, shaken to the point of indescribable sorrow. It was especially difficult for me to relive the pain of my own accounts. The memories that came flooding back to me, of finding out about my father's life-threatening situation that night, the phone calls, the number of times doctors began to lose hope for a recovery all led to tear drops staining my keyboard. But it was well worth it. Months after commencing work in May 2015, my father's story is finally ready to be told. It has been long overdue.

I would like to use this space to express my profound gratitude to those who played a role, small or big, in this saga: the strangers that found my father in the middle of the road; Sharjah police; the medical staff across all the hospitals who worked tirelessly to ensure his survival, whether directly or indirectly; the people and organizations involved in getting hospital transfers approved; my parents' places of work, for their unceasing financial support; and of course, my extensive circle of family and friends for your ardent prayers for my father's full recovery...wherever you are, know that you are one of the reasons he has been able to provide me with a narrative for this book. Without your combined efforts, I may very well have been fatherless today, in which case things would have turned out very differently in regards to this publication. Go in grace.

Upholding the culture of the United Arab Emirates, I'd like to end with the Islamic greeting, *As-salamu* - " السلام عليكم و رحمة اللة و بركاتـةو "

alaykum wa rahmatu'llahi wa barakaatuhu - may the peace, mercy and blessings of God be upon you.

Ardavan Pervaiz Taraporewala

Author's Note

Trauma Redefined was never written with the intention of traumatizing the reader in any way. It is simply a narration of a chain of unfortunate, sometimes seemingly bizarre events. But however impossible they may seem, the happenings contained in this book, from the out-of-body experiences to the hallucinations, have been entirely and accurately documented, without the addition of the slightest falsehood. I hope it also serves as a warning: this can happen to *anyone*, and not everyone might be as lucky as I was to live to tell the tale. A split second is all it takes for fate to challenge you to a game of life and death.

I took a lot away from this experience; I learnt about the importance of positive thinking, understood that life was a gift that was not meant to be taken for granted, and most importantly,

I understood the significance of family time. Before the incident, I used to live a very fast-paced life. I'd reach work at 8:00a.m, come home at around 5:30p.m, kiss the family, shower, and be out the door again, on my way to a club, movie or restaurant with friends. I'd arrive home as late as 4:00a.m at times, and then be up again by 6:00a.m for work, without a hint of tiredness in my eyes. The week would continue like this, and come Friday, I'd recharge my batteries by sleeping for almost the entire day, waking up only for meals. My friends often advised me to take it slower, maybe get a little more sleep at night, but my response would always be, "Who needs sleep? There's plenty of time for that when you're dead."

I've realized what happened to me was no coincidence. It was, I truly believe, God Himself telling me that I needed to hit the brakes and move out of the fast lane. My life did almost come to a screeching halt and recovery was an excruciatingly slow process, and the two combined taught me a valuable lesson: cramming everything into your daily schedule, trying to do too much, while at times admirable, can often lead to one not noticing or paying enough attention to the more important things in life-family, for example. I find myself spending more time with them now than I used to before the incident occurred, and I'm a better man for it. Sometimes, you just have to take things slowly, or you could very easily crash.

More importantly, I finally understood what my grandfather said when he told me, "Son, if ever you go out to seek revenge, please make sure you dig two graves." The second grave would belong to me. Had I exacted revenge on the driver who ran me over, how would that make me any different than him? Would I have been able to live with myself, with the guilt of hurting his family out of spite, the way he hurt mine? Additionally, if I were Hell-bent on getting revenge, the obsession with finding him would undoubtedly drive me insane, and distance myself from my family. It poisons the mind, body and soul, and consumes a human until there's nothing left.

I have but two regrets: first, being unable, while at Qassimi, to tell my family and friends that despite all the doctors' warnings, the fatal diseases I developed, and the physical damage I undertook, I *would* make it out of the ordeal alive. I wish I was able to provide them with the sense of surety and safety that God provided me.

And secondly, the names of the two men who found me on the pavement, and called the police and paramedics for me, have not been recorded in the book, not for identity protection purposes, but because they have both escaped my recollection. Sometimes, I am still left wondering as to whether they were even human. Why could they not be angels?

Speaking of angels, I would like to take this opportunity to introduce to you yet another angel God has brought into my life: Gulshat Jumayeva from Turkmenistan. An absolute gem, without a mean bone in her body, it was her resolute and firm relationship with God that touched me above everything else. The way she thought and spoke about her faith was a breath of fresh air, and the passion with which she'd narrate Biblical stories was endearing.

I brought her home to meet the family, and she took an instant fondness to my now late mother-in-law, Mehru, or 'Angel Mommy' as she would fondly call her. She refers to me as her elder brother, and affectionately calls me 'Brother Jaan', where 'Jaan' is a Farsi word, meaning 'dear'.

There are no *Atish Khadehs* (Fire Temples-Zoroastrian places of worship) in Dubai, so this one day, I asked her if I might accompany her to Church on Friday.

"Brother Jaan, you'd be more than welcome!" she exclaimed, absolutely delighted.

She took me to the United Christians Church, where the pastor's opening to the sermon was moving.

"Good morning, and welcome to the United Christians Church of Dubai. First and foremost, a very warm welcome to our non-Christian friends."

Ever since then, I've made every effort to go with Gulshat to church every Friday. It's an absolute joy to see a community worship so ardently, glorifying God through uplifting and beautiful music. Thank you, Gulshat, for providing me with this opportunity.

There are three people who were absolutely instrumental in the creating of this book. First and foremost, the driver who ran me over. I suppose there can be no story without him. He, like the angels who found me, shall remain anonymous; to this day, I don't know who he is, and there was not enough evidence for the police to go by in order to identify him and bring him to justice.

Second, the concerned authorities who decided my story was too harrowing to be recreated and aired on national television as was once intended, without any form of censorship. The producer of the show interviewed me, and even asked for copies of my X-rays to display on screen for the audience, which I was happy to provide her with. However, she called me a few days later, just when I thought things were finalized and the segment was going to be aired.

"I'm afraid the authorities feel your story is too harrowing for our home audiences, and your X-rays are extremely graphic. They're requesting censorship rights before we air anything."

"Madam," I replied, "if I were Jacob Grimm writing about Snow White's adventures in the forest, or Walt Disney narrating about Uncle Donald's skiing trip, you would have had my permission to change and censor the story to your heart's content. But my story is true, down to the finest detail, and if I'm to tell it, I want nothing left out. If we cannot agree on that, please do not bother airing it at all."

With that, the entire segment of the show on which my story was meant to be told was scrapped. Had this not taken place, and if my story had been aired, I might not have been motivated to write a book, for my tale would already have been told.

And finally, my son Ardavan, who spent a large portion of the summer of 2015 working on this project, turning my recollections, and those of my wife and daughter, into cohesive prose. Without his hard work, diligence and attention to detail, this book would never have been possible. Endless thanks, my son. May God bless and watch over you, always.

Pervaiz Taraporewala